HELP—MY CHILD IS BULLYING ME!
How to Stop Bullying at Home — Without Losing Your Mind, Your Faith, or Your Peace

by
Angela Saint
Angela Saint Media, LLC
Houston, Texas
AngelaSaint.com

Help—My Child Is Bullying Me!

© 2025 Angela Saint

All rights reserved

No part of this publication may be reproduced, stored in a retrieval system, or transmitted in any form or by any means—electronic, mechanical, photocopying, recording, or otherwise—without prior written permission from the publisher, except for brief quotations in reviews or other noncommercial uses permitted by copyright law.

Published by
Angela Saint Media, LLC
3139 W. Holcombe Blvd., Suite 2026
Houston, TX 77025 USA
AngelaSaint.com

Cover design: Angela Saint Brand Team
Interior design: Angela Saint Brand Team

All stories used in this book are composites, anonymized, or fictionalized to protect privacy. This book provides educational and inspirational guidance and is not legal, therapeutic, or medical advice.

ISBN: 978-8-9938342-0-7
Printed in the United States of America

DEDICATION

To every parent who has loved hard, prayed harder, and refused to let chaos raise their child — this book is for you. And to my own family: thank you for teaching me grace, grit, and the power of a calm spine.

"Boundaries start at hello."
— Saint Truth Bomb

AUTHOR'S NOTE

This book was born out of late nights, deep sighs, real stories, fierce prayers, and the unwavering belief that families can transform — not by force, but by clarity, consistency, and calm leadership.

Every example, every tool, every truth bomb in these pages comes from decades of parenting, educating, and walking beside parents who knew they were meant for more peace than the chaos they were tolerating.

If any chapter in this book made you feel seen, strengthened, or steadied, then my mission is complete.

You're not alone.
You're not failing.
You're rising — and your home will rise with you.

— **Angela Saint**

Table of Contents

INTRODUCTION	X
CHAPTER ONE	1
CHAPTER TWO	21
CHAPTER THREE	35
CHAPTER FOUR	57
CHAPTER FIVE	73
CHAPTER SIX	88
CHAPTER SEVEN	106
CHAPTER EIGHT	118
CHAPTER NINE	133
CHAPTER TEN	145

CHAPTER ELEVEN	162
CHAPTER TWELVE	177
CHAPTER THIRTEEN	200
CHAPTER FOURTEEN	223
CHAPTER FIFTEEN	239
CHAPTER SIXTEEN	259
CHAPTER SEVENTEEN	277
CHAPTER EIGHTEEN	295
CHAPTER NINETEEN	308
CHAPTER TWENTY	326
CHAPTER TWENTY-ONE	342
CHAPTER TWENTY-TWO	350

INTRODUCTION

The boundary dance starts early

Every parent enters the journey imagining peaceful mornings and respectful children who "yes ma'am" their way through life. And then reality knocks:
A toddler tests limits.
A teen rolls eyes.
An adult child demands benefits with none of the respect.

Disrespect doesn't arrive like a thunderstorm.
It starts as a drizzle.

A "hold on."
A "wait."
A "But why?"
A "That's stupid."

One day you wake up and realize—
Your child has become the loudest voice in the home,
and you're whispering in a house you pay for.

This book is your permission slip to step back into leadership with love, clarity, and a calm spine.

PART ONE

FOUNDATIONS: WHERE BOUNDARIES ARE BORN

CHAPTER ONE

The first fence: how early patterns shape the home

The first time I realized my "fence" had disappeared, my daughter was four.
Four — all cheeks and curly hair, with a voice like she'd swallowed a tiny bell.
Here's the secret parents rarely say out loud:
The first fences aren't built when your child is old enough to talk back — they're built when they're still small enough to sleep on your chest.

Before the eye-rolls.

Before the teenage tone.

Before the slammed doors.

Most of the bullying behaviors that explode at fifteen?

They first whispered at age three.

I remember the exact day it happened — my daughter, tiny, cute, and dangerously self-aware, looked me dead in my face, shook her head, and said:

"No."

Not playful.

Not confused.

A calculated no — the kind with strategy behind it.

And something in my spirit said,
"Pay attention, Dee. That's not a tantrum... that's a test."

In that moment, I realized something parents avoid admitting:

Kids are smart.
Smart enough to run test trials on your boundaries.
Smart enough to sense hesitation.
Smart enough to memorize where your "no" wiggles into a "fine, whatever."

Those tiny tests become patterns.
Those patterns become expectations.
Expectations become behavior.

That's why the early years matter so much — not because you can prevent every issue, but because your child is learning your leadership style long before they learn multiplication.

This is where the first fence stands… or cracks.

THE DAY THE FENCE FELL

It was a Tuesday morning.
I had laid out her clothes the night before — pink shirt, denim jumper, clean socks, shoes by the door. A full day ahead, no room for theatrics.

She walked in, placed her hand on her hip like she paid the mortgage, and said:

"No. I'm not wearing that."

Not a scream.
Not chaos.
Just a quiet rebellion so confident it froze me.

I tried everything — explaining, negotiating, sweet-talking.

Baby, she shut all that down.

And instead of holding the line, I panicked.

I didn't want her upset.
Didn't want the morning derailed.
Didn't want the daycare judgment.
Didn't want the fight.

So what did I do?

I caved.
Not once.
Not twice.
Every morning for a week.

By Friday, she had a whole runway show in the hallway — mixing fabrics, matching nothing, wearing rainboots in July. She was the stylist, the executive producer, and the boss of her own little reality show while I stood there…

an underpaid intern.

Before that moment, I believed a firm tone and steady hand were enough to anchor a household. But that deliberate "No" showed me how quickly the balance can shift — how a single blurred line becomes a blueprint a child follows faithfully.

Each compromise carved out new territory.
Each negotiation taught her my "no" had an escape hatch.
Each soft answer rewrote my authority.

That week became a masterclass in the quiet power of consistency.

With every wobble, I wasn't preserving peace —
I was training her to expect negotiation instead of leadership.

THE TRUTH ABOUT EARLY BEHAVIOR

Here's the part that stings:

She didn't become disrespectful overnight.
I trained her to expect flexibility where there should've been clarity.

Kids don't need perfection.
They need predictability.

If "no" becomes "sometimes,"
"later" becomes "never,"
and "stop" becomes "just this once,"
your child pushes not because they're bad —

but because the fence is invisible.

Kids test boundaries to find safety, not power.

When a child knows:

"This is the line."
"This is the limit."
"This is the rule."

They relax.
They settle.
They trust.

Because clarity is comfort.

A wobbly fence?
Oh, they'll push it until it falls on top of you.

EARLY SIGNS OF BULLYING BEHAVIORS (MOST PARENTS MISS THEM)

These are not dramatic moments.
They're micro-moves with major impact.

1. The Selective Hearing Routine

You say, "Come here."
They suddenly go deaf.
Not medically — strategically.

2. The Micro-Negotiator

"Five more minutes?"
"One more show?"
"I'll do it later."

Tiny sentences, big training.

3. The Silent Standoff

You ask them to put on shoes.
They sit… quietly… calculating your next move.

4. The Third-Party Appeal

You say no.
They ask Daddy, Grandma, Auntie, the neighbor's dog.

5. The Toy Hostage Situation

Taking something that's not theirs and calling it "sharing."

None of these make your child "bad."
They make them human.

Your job isn't to eliminate the push —
it's to stay the fence.

THE DEVELOPMENT ARC — HOW SMALL BEHAVIORS GROW UP

Early behaviors don't stay early.
They evolve.
They mature.
They grow teeth

Age 3–4: The Micro-Tests

- Selective hearing
- "I said no" experiments
- Quiet resistance wrapped in cuteness

They're not challenging authority — they're mapping it.

Age 6–8: The Pattern Stage

If the early tests go unchecked, the behavior graduates. Now you see:
- "I forgot."
- "You didn't tell me."
- "I'll do it later."

They're using the blueprint you handed them.

Age 9–12: The Tone Shift

Suddenly the behaviors come with volume.
- Eye rolls
- Sighs
- "Why do I have to?"

This isn't new —
it's the same fence wobbling, now with a microphone.

Age 13–15: The Power Phase

When the fence stays weak, strategy kicks in.
- Selective compliance
- Emotional shutdowns
- Arguing every rule
- Performing for one parent, resisting the other

Parents ask, "Where did this come from?"
But it started in the little places we let slide.

Age 16–18: The Gray-Haired Toddler Stage

Now they use leverage:
- Gaslighting lite
- Guilt
- Weaponized independence
- "I'm grown."

Living at your address doesn't make you grown.
Grown boundaries do.

And here's the hope:
At ANY stage, the fence can be rebuilt.

Kids adapt to clarity fast.
They rise when you rise.

THE PATTERN STARTS QUIETLY

A slammed door starts as a sigh.
A disrespectful tone starts as a shrug.
A refusal starts as a negotiation.

Bullying at home rarely erupts suddenly.
It forms in the small moments we excuse away.

The first fence isn't built with force.
It's built with consistency.

Not shouting.
Not threatening.
Not overexplaining.

Just calm, predictable leadership.

A predictable parent creates a peaceful home.

THE FENCES WE INHERITED (GENERATIONAL PATTERNS)

Before you blame yourself, pause.

Some fences you're trying to build...
you never saw modeled.

Most of us parent with blueprints we didn't choose.

Rigid fences:
- "Because I said so."
- "Children are seen, not heard."
- Discipline without dialogue.

No fences:
- Adults afraid of conflict
- Apologizing to the child
- Chaos mistaken for freedom

Moving fences:
- Boundaries changed with moods
- Leadership depended on stress
- Consequences came unpredictably

You cannot maintain a fence you never learned to build.
Not because you're weak —
because you're human.

Everything you observed growing up…
Tone.
Disrespect.
Consequences.
Boundaries.
Leadership.

You absorbed all of it before you could spell your name.

Generational patterns don't break because of intention.
They break because of awareness.

Awareness gives you authority.

You are the generation that says:
"The fence will not wobble another decade."
"This pattern stops in my house."
"My kids will know leadership AND love."

You're not just rebuilding a fence —
you're rebuilding the family tree

THE MOMENT I REALIZED I WAS PARENTING FROM MY PAST

It happened when my daughter was eight.

She pushed a small boundary — nothing that should've triggered me. But something rose up in my chest that didn't belong to the moment.

My voice sharpened.
My posture stiffened.
My spirit braced itself.

And I heard my grandmother's voice:

"Don't let these kids run over you."

But nobody was running over me.
I was running from my own childhood.

I paused — mid-sentence — and stepped back inside myself.

I remembered being little...
scared to speak...
wishing for a parent who would talk *to* me, not *at* me.

I knelt beside her and said:

"Give me a moment. I want to talk to you the way I needed someone to talk to me."

That day, the room shifted.
I shifted.

Because you cannot parent in the present while dragging the fears of the past.

You have to notice them.
Name them.
Choose differently.

And choosing differently is the real generational curse-breaker.

TRANSITION PARAGRAPH

Even after all that reflection, knowing better doesn't mean doing better — not at first. Growth shows up in real life, not theory. And sometimes the universe gives you a second test just to make sure you meant what you said about tightening that fence.

THE MORNING I DECIDED TO STOP LOSING TO A TODDLER

The next week, God handed me Round Two of the "Who Runs This House?" Olympics — this time with an audience.

My daughter emerged wearing:
- mismatched socks
- a glitter tutu
- my church shoes (reserved for Easter and funerals only)

She twirled like she was auditioning for a Broadway revival of Chaos: The Musical.

Then, with the confidence of a woman paying rent, she said:

"I'm wearing this today."

Old me would've negotiated myself into a migraine.

But that morning, something clicked.

I remembered the fence.
The peace I was trying to build.
And the undeniable truth:

A four-year-old should not be out here beating me in mental chess.

So I breathed — long, grown-woman, "Jesus be a fence" breath — and said:

"Sweetheart, you can wear the tutu after school.
For school, it's the outfit on the bed."

She froze.
Face crumpled.
Pre-cry inhale loading.

I stayed steady.

Not harsh.
Not cold.
Just unmoved.

She tried again, louder.

"No! I want THIS!"

I said the line that changed everything:

"I hear you.
And the answer is still no."

— the silence?
You would've thought I unplugged the Wi-Fi.

She stomped.
She pouted.
She folded her arms until her shoulders touched.

But I stayed the fence.

Five minutes later?

She walked out in the outfit I chose —
tutu tucked in her backpack for after-school flare.

And as she grabbed my hand, she sighed — the soft kind that says:

"Whew... somebody's in charge. Thank God."

That moment was tiny.
But it became a turning point.

Kids bloom when leadership is steady and love is consistent.

I didn't just rebuild the fence for her.
I rebuilt it for the little girl inside me who never had one.

TRUTH BOMB

Kids don't need a perfect parent — just one who doesn't fold under a four-year-old with glitter and a dream.

REFLECT & RESET

REFLECT:
Where have I been negotiating with a child who simply needed leadership?

RESET:
What's one decision I will stand firm on this week — calmly, kindly, consistently?

LEGACY:
How will my consistency today shape the emotional climate of my home tomorrow?

SAINT LINE

A steady parent grows a steady child. Fence first — peace follows.

CLOSING TRANSITION

That morning didn't magically fix everything — but it shifted everything.
Once the fence stood firm for even five minutes, the atmosphere in our home began to recalibrate. Respect doesn't return in lightning strikes — it comes through small, repeated choices that tell your child:

"You're safe. I'm steady. We're good."

From that day forward, rebuilding boundaries felt less like a battle and more like a blessing — the quiet work of a parent reclaiming peace, tone, and leadership.

FIRST FENCE MISTAKES MOST PARENTS MAKE

Confusing kindness with negotiation.

Over-explaining a simple boundary.

Delaying consequences until they lose power.

Rewarding cooperation after a meltdown.

Asking for opinions instead of giving direction.

Expecting calm while modeling chaos.

Letting exhaustion rewrite the standard.

Treating early sass as "cute."

Allowing Grandma/Daddy/Auntie to override your "no."

Believing respect is automatic rather than taught.

THE FENCE REBUILDS WITH ONE DECISION

Children feel safest when the parent decides:

"I lead. You follow with love."

Not dictatorship.
Not fear.
Just steady, predictable leadership.

Leadership says:
"I hear you."
"I love you."
"And the answer is still no."

Leadership is calm, not loud.
Firm, not cold.
Consistent, not controlling.

When you reclaim your fence?

Chaos packs its bags.

Consistency is the oxygen of early boundaries.

REAL-TIME FENCE TOOL (LIVE EXAMPLE)

A few days later, the universe tested me again — as always.

Saturday morning.
My daughter wanted to go out wearing two skirts, one boot, and a pajama top that had fought the dryer and lost.

Old me:
"Why would you wear—"

Fence-Rebuilt Me:
Ten-word rule. Calm voice.

"Choose the blue shirt or the red shirt — that's it."

She blinked, calculating.
Then tried her classic stall:

"But I don't want—"

I didn't budge.

Calm Countdown:
"Five… four…"

By "three," she grabbed the red shirt like a peace treaty.

Her shoulders softened.
Breathing settled.
She relaxed.

Because clarity calms kids.

Later she crawled in my lap and whispered:

"Mommy, I like when you talk like that."

Look at God.

Kids don't fight fences that make them feel safe.
They fight confusion.

AUDIT

- Where is my first fence wobbling?
- What small behavior am I negotiating instead of leading?
- What ONE boundary will I reinforce today — calmly?

PRAYER

Lord, help me rebuild the first fence with wisdom, love, and steady strength.
Give me clarity when I wobble and confidence when I feel unsure.
Help my child feel safe inside the structure I create.
Amen.

FINAL SAINT LINE

Rebuild the first fence, and the whole house stands taller.

CHAPTER TWO
The mirror test: healing the parent before the child

Parenting exposes the parts of us we thought we buried.

The fears.
The insecurities.
The childhood wounds.
The "I'll never do what my mama did" vows we whispered at fifteen.

All of it rises to the surface the moment you try to parent another human being.

People think parenting is about raising a child.
They don't tell you it's also about meeting the unhealed version of yourself — over and over again.

Your child slams a door, and suddenly you're back in your childhood bedroom.
Your teen rolls their eyes, and you hear your mother's tone coming out of your own mouth.
Your toddler screams "NO!", and your chest tightens in a way that has nothing to do with preschool and everything to do with how you were treated when you were small.

Parenting is a mirror.
A relentless one.

Sometimes it reflects the best of you — your patience, your humor, your tenderness.

But other times, it drags old pain to the surface like a song you didn't ask to hear again.

Healing isn't linear, especially when you're parenting through your own unfinished business. There are moments that catch you off guard — when your child's behavior hits a bruise you didn't know was still there, and suddenly you're not just a parent… you're the wounded child all over again, standing in the same emotional kitchen, hearing echoes from decades before.

That's the mirror test.

It's not a punishment.
It's an invitation.

An invitation to pause.
To look inward.
To ask, "Is this really about my child… or is this about me?"

When Your Child Sounds Like Your Past

Sometimes the hardest part of parenting isn't your child's behavior — it's realizing your reaction is coming from a place much older than they are.

The sharp tone that jumps out of your mouth.
The shutdown that happens when your child talks back.
The way you over-explain, over-punish, or over-react — not because of what they did, but because of what you never got.

It sneaks up on you in the most regular moments:

Your child says, "You never listen to me," and something in you flares — not because they're wrong, but because you grew up feeling unheard.

Your teen mutters, "You're doing too much," and suddenly you are seven again, being told you were "too sensitive" or "too dramatic" for having normal feelings.

Your toddler screams in the grocery store, and the embarrassment in your body feels bigger than the aisle you're standing in — because deep down, you still remember what it felt like to be shamed in public.

This is the mirror test:
Your child's behavior taps the same nerve your past never soothed.

That realization can be jarring. But it's also powerful.

Because once you recognize, *"Oh, this is old,"* you stop fighting the child in front of you and start tending to the child inside of you.

Healing as a parent doesn't mean pretending, you're fine. It means being honest enough to say:

"That comment hurt more than it should have."

"My reaction is bigger than this moment."

"Something in me is asking to be healed."

You don't fail the mirror test by feeling triggered.
You fail it by refusing to look.

The Day the Mirror Got Loud

The mirror had been whispering for years.
That day, it finally shouted.

My daughter was sixteen — full teenage form, walking around like she was the star of a show I didn't audition for. She had been snapping at everybody, rolling her eyes, sighing like breathing was manual labor.

I called her into the kitchen and said, "We need to talk."

She looked me dead in my face and said:

"I don't feel like talking."

Not loud.
Not screaming.
Just flat. Dismissive. Done.

And that dismissiveness?
It hit me in a place that had nothing to do with her and everything to do with me.

Immediately, I felt something rising in my chest:

It was old.
It was deep.
It was familiar.

It was the little girl inside me who had been dismissed more times than she could count. The one who was told, "Go somewhere, I'm tired," or "Not right now, I'm busy," or "You doing too much."

In that moment, I wasn't reacting to my daughter.
I was reacting to years of not being heard.

The urge in my body was strong:

Prove you're in charge.

Shut this down.

Make sure she never talks to you like that again.

I could feel myself about to raise my voice — not as a parent leading her child, but as a wounded girl fighting not to be pushed aside one more time.

And right there, in the middle of my own kitchen, the mirror test showed up with a microphone.

A thought slid in, quiet but clear:

"She is not your enemy.
She is not the one who hurt you.
Don't make her pay for a bill she didn't create."

I had to swallow one of the hardest truths I've ever faced:

Sometimes your child isn't triggering you.
They're revealing you.

She wasn't my problem.
My unhealed places were.

WHY THE MIRROR TEST MATTERS

Children reflect us — not to embarrass us, but to awaken us.

The mirror test asks:

"What is my child pulling out of me that still needs healing?"

Sometimes you aren't yelling because of your child. You're yelling because:

You were silenced growing up and you promised yourself no one would ever disrespect you again.

You were constantly corrected and now you over-correct to avoid feeling out of control.

You were the peacemaker in your family and conflict still terrifies you.

You never saw healthy boundaries modeled, so everything feels like either a fight or a surrender.

Your child did not create the wound.
They simply touched it.

If you don't understand that, you'll spend your parenting years fighting the wrong enemy.

You'll think:

"My child is so disrespectful,"
when really, your past is unhealed.

"My teen makes me feel small,"
when really, you never learned how to feel grounded in your own voice.

"I'm failing as a parent,"
when really, you're being invited to heal as a person.

The mirror test is not about guilt.
It's about awareness.

And awareness is what gives you choice.

BREAKING THE CYCLE (WITHOUT BREAKING YOURSELF)

You cannot parent from a place you've never healed.

If you try, your home becomes a wrestling match between your present intentions and your past pain.

The mirror test gives you a chance to step off that treadmill and say:

I'm not parenting from fear today.

I'm not parenting from my childhood today.

I'm not parenting from guilt today.

I am parenting from clarity today.

Clarity doesn't mean you feel nothing.
It means you notice what you feel and decide what to do with it.

When you start choosing clarity:

You stop taking every comment as an attack.

You stop treating every boundary as a war.

You stop over-giving to make up for what you didn't have.

Your healing shifts the entire home.

A regulated parent creates a regulated household.
A parent who can pause, breathe, and reset gives their child something many of us never had:

Emotional safety.

Not perfection.
Not a parent who never yells.
A parent who knows how to say:

"I didn't like how I handled that. Let's try again."

That alone breaks more generational patterns than any speech.

THE HEALING CONVERSATION (WHAT I DID DIFFERENTLY)

Back to that kitchen.

Sixteen-year-old attitude.
Forty-something-year-old trigger.

Everything in me wanted to prove a point.
To say, "Excuse me? Who do you think you're talking to?" with a side of volume and a list of consequences.

But the mirror test had me by the shoulders.

So I did something I wasn't raised to do:

I paused.

I took a breath — a long, grown-woman breath — and silently asked myself:

"What is this really about? Her... or me?"

The answer was obvious.
This was about me.

So instead of snapping back, I chose a different script.

I said, calmly:

"We're not talking like this.
We'll talk when we're both calmer.
Disrespect is not an option in this house.
We'll try again in 20 minutes."

No yelling.
No lecture.
No tit-for-tat.

Just a clear boundary and a built-in reset.

She stomped off at first — still in teenage form.
But twenty minutes later, she came back downstairs softer.

Not perfect.
Not suddenly healed.
But reachable.

We talked.
She shared what was really going on underneath the attitude.
I admitted I had almost slipped into my old patterns.

And in that moment, I realized something:

Sometimes the healing isn't in your child changing. It's in you stepping out of your old story.

The mirror test had done its job.

HOW TO USE THE MIRROR TEST IN REAL LIFE

Here's the practical version — because you don't need another theory; you need tools for Tuesday at 7:13 p.m. when someone slams a door.

1. Pause the Reaction

Before you correct your child, catch yourself.

Ask:

"What am I feeling in my body right now?"

"Does this feeling belong 100% to this moment... or does it feel familiar from my past?"

If it feels bigger than the moment, it's not just about your child.

2. Name the Trigger

You don't have to unpack your whole childhood on the spot. But you can name the trigger to yourself:

"I feel dismissed."

"I feel disrespected."

"I feel unseen."

"I feel like I did as a child."

Naming it shrinks it.
What we don't name, controls us.
What we name, we can steward.

3. Lead From Calm, Not Chaos

Once you see the trigger, you can choose your response.

That might sound like:

"I'm not going to yell, even though I want to."

"I'm going to set a boundary without recreating how I was treated."

"We're going to pause this conversation and come back to it."

You're still the parent.
You're still the leader.
You're just leading from healing, not from hurt.

That's the mirror test in action.

AUDIT

- What parts of my past show up most when I'm disciplining my child?
- Where am I reacting instead of leading?
- What old story — "I'm helpless," "I'm disrespected," "I'm failing" — do I need to release so I can parent from strength?

PRAYER

Lord, shine a gentle light on the wounds I still carry.
Heal the places in me that make my parenting shaky.
Help me pause before I react, and respond with wisdom instead of old scripts.
Teach me to lead my child from a healed place, not a hurting one.
Amen.

TRUTH BOMB

Parenting exposes the wounds you never healed — not to shame you, but so you can finally heal them.

REFLECT & RESET

REFLECT:
Where did my child recently trigger a reaction that felt bigger

than the situation? What old memory or feeling was really underneath it?

RESET:

What is one simple phrase I can use this week to pause the moment — like, "We'll talk when we're calm," or "Give me a second to think"?

LEGACY:

If my child grows up watching me own my triggers and choose calmer responses, what will that teach them about apologies, boundaries, and healing?

FINAL SAINT LINE

Heal you — and your child will rise with you.

CHAPTER THREE
Calm leadership: stepping into your role without guilt

Your calm is the loudest authority your child will ever hear.

Your child doesn't need a louder parent.
Your child needs a steadier parent.

We live in a world that worships volume. Whoever yells the loudest, posts the most, or claps back the fastest is seen as "in control." But in a healthy home, real authority doesn't sound like a megaphone.

It sounds like calm.

Calm isn't passive.
Calm isn't weak.
Calm is controlled strength.

True calm leadership starts with a quiet confidence in your own authority — a steady belief that you don't have to yell to be heard or control every detail to be respected. When you lead with calm, you send a clear message:

Problems can be handled without panic. Feelings are allowed, but they are not driving this house.

That steadiness becomes the anchor your child looks for, especially when the emotional weather turns stormy.

Kids push hardest when they sense uncertainty.
But when your energy is grounded, their chaos slowly loses air.

What Calm Leadership Really Is

Let's clear this up:

Calm is not soft.

Calm is not permissive.

Calm is not silence.

Calm is a position.

Calm says, "I am the leader here."
Not through force, but through stability.

Think of your home like a room with a thermostat and a smoke alarm.

Yelling is the smoke alarm — loud, panicked, reactive.
Calm leadership is the thermostat — steady, intentional, quietly setting the temperature.

When you show up steady, your child learns:

We can disagree without disaster.

We can be corrected without being crushed.

We can feel big feelings without burning the whole house down.

Calm is not the absence of emotion.
Calm is emotion under leadership.

You Set the Weather

Here's the part most parents overlook: calm isn't a reaction. Calm is a decision you make ahead of time.

Kids don't wake up choosing chaos — they wake up checking your weather report.

If you come in stormy, they brace for lightning.

If you come in scattered, they scatter.

If you come in anchored, they settle.

Calm leadership means you quietly decide:

"The weather in this house starts with me."

Your tone becomes the thermostat.
Your presence becomes home base.
Your consistency becomes the safety net they didn't know they needed.

Children — even the grown ones — study your emotional patterns like a blueprint. They are constantly, silently asking:

How loud is too loud?

How far can I push before the walls move?

Will Mom follow through or fold?

Does she mean what she says, or is this just another speech?

Calm leadership removes the guessing game.

It says, "This is who I am every day. You don't have to gamble."

When you become predictable:

Their anxiety goes down.

Their resistance softens.

Their respect grows — not because you're scary, but because you are steady.

Three Everyday Pictures of Calm Leadership

Let's bring this down to ground level. Calm leadership isn't theory — it's Tuesday afternoon.

Example 1: The Bedroom Explosion

Your teen's room looks like a crime scene.
Clothes everywhere.

Old food on the nightstand.
Shoes hiding like they're in witness protection.

Old you would storm in yelling:

"This room is a disaster! You don't care about anything!"

Calm leadership says:

"Your room needs to be cleaned by 6 PM. I'll check then."

No debate.
No pleading.
No emotional hurricane.

The message: This is the standard. This is the time. I trust you to handle it.

Kids respond better to clarity than to chaos.

Example 2: The Attitude Olympics

You ask for help.
They sigh, roll their eyes, and make that face.

Old you:

"You don't pay any bills! You're so ungrateful!"

Calm leadership says:

"You can have an attitude or you can have privileges — but not both."

Delivered gently.
Delivered once.
Delivered like policy, not punishment.

The energy in the room shifts. Leadership resets it — without raising your voice.

Example 3: The Public Embarrassment Panic

You're in public.
Your child starts putting on a show because they assume you won't react the same in front of people.

Old you:

"Fine. Just this once. We'll talk at home."

(And if we're honest, the talk at home never comes.)

Calm leadership says:

"We'll finish this in private. But the answer is still no."

Not angry.
Not embarrassed.
Just consistent.

Kids relax when your energy predicts your response — in public and in private.

Why Calm Feels So Hard

Calm sounds beautiful on paper...
right up until someone slams a door, rolls their eyes, or hits you with:

"I'm not doing that."

Let's be real:
Calm isn't natural. Calm is trained.

Calm grows in the tiny gap between what just happened and how you choose to respond.

Most parents lose calm for three big reasons:

1. You're Tired

Worn-out people don't lead well.
Exhaustion steals patience, creativity, and perspective.

When you're drained, everything feels like disrespect — even when it's not.

2. You're Triggered

Kids don't know your wounds, but they always manage to bump into them.

A tone.

A look.

A comment that sounds like someone from your past.

Suddenly you're reacting to 1998, not 2025.

3. You're Rushed

You're already late.

Dinner's not done.

Your phone is buzzing.

Now a child adds attitude on top?

Chaos multiplies where there is no margin.

Calm leadership doesn't ignore these realities. It simply refuses to let them drive.

Because when you lose calm, your child loses direction.
When you regain calm, your child regains trust.

The Power of the Pause

Calm leadership does not mean standing there like a statue.

It means using the pause as your power move.

Before you respond:

Exhale once — slowly.

Drop your shoulders.

Lower your voice on purpose.

Say less — but mean all of it.

The pause communicates three things:

I'm not rattled by your behavior.

I have options besides yelling.

I choose strategy over chaos.

Kids are used to volume. Calm throws them off — in a holy way.

The silence tells the truth your mouth hasn't spoken yet: "I'm in control of me. You don't get to drive my reactions."

The Secret: Calm Doesn't Lower Consequences — It Clarifies Them

Some parents hear "calm" and think "lenient."

No, baby. Calm doesn't mean you soften the standard.

Calm means you stick to it.

A calm parent follows through.
A panicked parent negotiates.

Calm consequences are:

Short

Clear

Connected to the behavior

Examples:

"If the room isn't clean by 6 PM, the phone is parked until tomorrow."

"With that tone, this conversation is paused until your voice matches your age."

"No chores, no Wi-Fi. That's the house policy."

You're not attacking their worth.
You're reinforcing the structure.

Calm turns consequences into predictable math — not emotional warfare.

The goal is not to scare your child.
The goal is to help them learn that stability feels safer than manipulation

Case Study: The Sunday Morning Meltdown

Let's walk through a real-life moment.

You say:

"We're leaving in five minutes."

Your daughter:

"No I'm not."

Your son:

"Where's my cereal? Why didn't you buy the good kind?"

Your spouse gives you *that* look — the "please handle this" look.

Old you would:

Yell

Rush

Threaten

Cry in the car

Calm leadership you do something different.

You kneel to eye level and say:

"Everyone needs to be in the car by 8:45.
If you're not ready, you'll go as you are."

Then you walk away.

No repeating yourself sixteen times.
No negotiating outfits.
No matching their chaos.

They throw mini-fits.
You stay steady.

When 8:45 hits?

You honor your word.

Messy hair? Mismatched clothes?
They go as they are.

Natural consequences are undefeated.

That is calm leadership:
Not loud. Not cruel. Just steady.

Why Kids Test Calm

Kids test consistency the same way you check a chair before you sit down — to see if it will hold.

They're not always trying to break you.
They're checking: *"Can I trust you?"*

When your calm becomes reliable:

They stop trying to out-argue you.

They stop using volume as leverage.

They stop assuming your "no" means "convince me."

They don't magically love every boundary.
But they know what to expect.

And predictable boundaries create safer kids — even if they groan all the way through them.

The Leadership Triangle: What Your Child Is Watching

Your child studies three things more than your words:

1. Your Face

Before you speak, your expression tells the story.

If you look scared, they push.

If you look furious, they defend.

If you look steady, they soften — even if they don't admit it.

2. Your Tone

Your tone answers the question:

"Are you the thermostat or the smoke alarm?"

Kids don't need constant sirens.
They need anchors.

A calm tone says, "I'm not going anywhere. The standard isn't either."

3. Your Follow-Through

Your credibility as a parent lives in your follow-through.

If you say 6 PM, mean 6 PM.

If you say "pause," then actually pause.

If you say, "that's enough," then stop explaining.

Leadership is not loud.
Leadership is consistent.

Calm Leadership in Real Life: Five Scenarios

Use these as templates you can adjust to your home.

Scenario 1: The Door Slam

Child: SLAMS the door so hard it shakes.

Old you:

"Oh REALLY? Now you've lost your mind!"

Calm you:

"That behavior tells me you need space.
The door stays open for the next 24 hours."

Short. Clear. Calm. Done.

Scenario 2: The Homework Refusal

Child:

"I'm not doing this."

Old you:

"Yes, you are! Sit down RIGHT NOW!"

Calm you:

"Homework has to be done before screens. When you're ready to begin, I'll help."

Then you walk away.
You offered structure, not a showdown.

Scenario 3: Talking Back

Child:

"Why do you always bother me? Just leave me alone!"

Calm you:

"I don't respond to disrespect. Try again with a calmer voice."

You don't reward poor communication with attention. You let them know the door to relationship is open — but disrespect doesn't walk through it.

Scenario 4: Grocery Store Meltdown

Child decides aisle 7 is the stage.

Old you: whispering through clenched teeth, bargaining, threatening.

Calm you:

"We're leaving the store.
We'll try again when you're able to shop respectfully."

Embarrassment shrinks when you remember:
You're raising a future adult, not auditioning for approval from strangers.

Scenario 5: The Silent Treatment

Child ignores you for hours because they didn't like a boundary.

Old you:

"Talk to me! Why are you acting like this?"

Calm you:

"I'm here when you're ready to communicate respectfully."

Your calm becomes the invitation.
Your steadiness becomes the lesson.

The Trigger Check: When You're About to Lose It

Your body will always tell you before your mouth does.

Look for:

Tight jaw

Racing heart

Shallow breathing

Fast, clipped words

A rising urge to "win" the moment

These are not signs that you're a bad parent.
They are signs that old patterns are waking up.

Calm leadership doesn't pretend you're not triggered.
It helps you say:

"I feel myself getting hot. Let me pause before I speak."

Then you reset:

Pause.

Breathe.

Lower your voice.

Continue.

Your child learns emotional regulation from the way you handle your own.

Five Sentences Every Calm Leader Uses

Keep these in your pocket. Use as needed:

"I'm not raising my voice. I'm raising my standards."

"We can talk — but only respectfully."

"I'm not arguing. I've made my decision."

"We'll pause this conversation until we're both calm."

"You can choose your behavior, or I'll choose the consequence."

These five alone can shift the entire atmosphere of your home.

The Truth About Guilt

Guilt feels like compassion, but it leads like chaos.

Guilt makes you:

Over-explain

Over-give

Over-apologize

Over-function

And under-lead.

Guilt says:

"Let me fix this so you won't be upset with me."

Leadership says:

"I love you too much to let chaos run this house."

Calm leadership doesn't ignore your compassion. It puts your compassion in partnership with boundaries — not in competition with them.

When Calm Feels Impossible

Some days, calm feels like climbing a mountain in flip-flops.

Those are the days your child needs your steadiness the most.

When you want to explode... whisper.
When you want to argue... pause.
When you want to give in... follow through.

Great leadership is not built in easy moments.
It's forged in the messy ones.

And your child is taking notes every time.

The 30-Day Calm Challenge: What Changes If You Commit

If you commit to practicing calm leadership for even 30 days — imperfectly, with grace — you will start to notice:

Fewer arguments

Softer tone from your child

Clearer boundaries

Less guilt-driven parenting

More cooperation

Stronger mutual respect

Your child may never say, "Thank you for being so calm, Mother of the Year."

But their behavior will tell on them.
Their nervous system will tell on them.
The peace in your home will tell on them.

Calm leadership is one of the greatest gifts you will ever give your family — and yourself.

REFLECT & RESET

REFLECT:
Where do I most often lose my calm — mornings, homework, chores, money, or bedtime? What usually sets me off?

RESET:

What is one phrase or script I will use this week *instead* of yelling or over-explaining? (Example: "We'll try this again when we're both calm.")

LEGACY:

If my child grows up remembering me as steady instead of explosive, how will that change the kind of parent they become one day?

AUDIT

- Where does guilt weaken my leadership?
- Do I speak with certainty or with apology?
- What is one area where I need to re-establish calm authority this week?

PRAYER

God, help me lead without guilt, fear, or frustration.
Give me a steady spirit and a clear voice.
Teach me to pause before I react,
to choose strategy over chaos,
and to let my calm become my authority.
Amen.

TRUTH BOMB

Calm isn't quiet — it's control.

FINAL SAINT LINE

Lead calmly today, and your home will breathe easier tomorrow.

CHAPTER FOUR
Slay the dragon, not your family

Every home has a moment when the argument stops being about the socks on the floor or the attitude in the doorway... and becomes about something deeper — the dragon in the room.

You know the dragon.

The tension that grows teeth.
The pattern that repeats like a bad rerun.
The storm that shows up even when nobody was fighting five minutes ago.

Here's the truth every calm leader eventually learns:

If you don't name the dragon, you'll start swinging at the people you love.

This chapter is about learning to separate your child from the chaos...
so you can fight the pattern, not the person.

SAINT SNAPSHOT: WHAT'S THE DRAGON?

THE DRAGON:
The repeating behavior cycle that hijacks your peace.
(Backtalk, negotiating, shutting down, escalating, deflecting.)

THE MISTAKE:
Thinking the child *is* the dragon.

THE TRUTH:

People aren't the problem — patterns are.

THE WIN:

When you shift focus from the child to the pattern, your home shifts from tension → teamwork.

WHEN THE ROOM FILLS WITH SMOKE

It was a Saturday evening when my daughter stormed into the living room, mumbling under her breath, irritated with the whole world — including me.

She wasn't yelling.
No profanity.
No slammed door.

But her energy?
Her energy walked in first.

Moments like this are where dragons thrive.
Not in the volume.
Not just in the words.
In the shift — the tension you feel before a sentence even lands.

Her frustration filled the room like smoke, swirling in the air, daring me to respond the old way: sharp tone, hands on hips, full cross-examination.

The dragon loves that.
It feeds on impulse.
It feasts on parents who react instead of lead.

But that night, something in me said, *"Not today."*

I lowered my voice.
Dropped my shoulders.
Shifted my breathing from fight mode to lead mode.

Not to win.
To break the cycle.

I focused on responding, not reacting — because the dragon feeds on reaction, but it starves on clarity.

I reminded myself:

Slay the dragon, not the child.

I softened my tone, not because I was backing down, but because calm is strategy.

Calm lowers the temperature.

Calm exposes the real issue.

Calm lets you see the pattern behind the behavior.

Her energy didn't disappear — dragons don't back down that easily.

But something small shifted:

Her shoulders dropped a quarter inch.

Her eyes flickered — confusion, maybe relief.

She hesitated instead of exploding.

And that's when I learned something sacred:

Kids don't fear boundaries. They fear uncertainty.
A steady parent makes the dragon retreat.

I sat steady.
Unmoved.
Not cold — anchored.

She watched to see if my calm was a trap.
If this new tone would wobble.
If the old mom would slip back out.

But I stayed consistent.
Not silent — *strategic*.

And slowly… the dragon loosened its grip on both of us.

ARE YOU FIGHTING TO BE RIGHT — OR TO RESTORE PEACE?

There's a moment in every conflict where you have a choice:

Am I fighting to be right?

Or am I fighting to restore peace?

Your child will reflect your posture before they respond to your words.

A calm parent is a lighthouse.
A reactive parent is a match.

One guides.
One burns.

That day, I refused to burn.

The dragon wanted fire.
It wanted me to meet attitude with attitude, sarcasm with sarcasm, volume with volume.

But I remembered:

The dragon wants fire, not solutions.
I don't have to give it oxygen.

So instead of escalating, I pivoted.

THE PIVOT MOMENT

"Don't start," she said when I gently asked, "What's going on?"

Old me would've snapped back,
"Oh, I'm starting. And you're about to finish."

But growth whispered, "Try something different."

So instead of rising up, I settled down.

I said, quietly:

"I'm not here to criticize. I just want to understand."

She blinked — thrown off.
Her shoulders shifted.
Her face softened, just enough to notice.

Calm confused the dragon.

It broke the rhythm.
It reset the board.

In that moment, I wasn't battling my daughter.
I was battling the pattern:

Misunderstanding

Escalation

Defensiveness

Distance

And by choosing presence over power, I cut off the dragon's fuel supply.

We didn't magically hug it out and start baking cookies.
We were still two humans with feelings and history.

But the air in that room changed.
You could feel it.

Sometimes the win is not a perfect ending.
Sometimes the win is less damage.

NAMING THE DRAGON

She wasn't the enemy.
The pattern was.

I took a breath, looked her in the eyes, and said:

"Let's pause.
We're not fighting each other.
We're fighting the dragon between us."

She frowned. "What dragon?"

"The pattern," I said.
"The part that wants us arguing instead of solving. The thing that shows up every time we're both tired, stressed, and not saying what we really mean."

She rolled her eyes a little, but she didn't walk away.

For the first time in a long time...
she softened.

Naming the dragon gave us both something to fight together instead of fighting each other.

That's the shift:

The child isn't the dragon. The pattern is.

THE FIVE DRAGONS THAT LIVE IN MOST HOMES

You can't slay what you won't name.
Let's call these dragons out.

1. The Backtalk Dragon

Snappy remarks.
Sarcastic tone.
Sharp sighs.

This dragon wants to turn every request into a disrespect show.

Slay it with:

"I hear you're frustrated. Tone still matters. Try again."

You're not ignoring the feeling — you're training the delivery.

2. The Negotiate-Everything Dragon

Every rule becomes a courtroom.

"But why?"

"Can we talk about it?"

"Just this one time?"

This dragon turns your home into Congress.

Slay it with:

"This is a decision, not a discussion. We're moving forward."

Not mean.
Not defensive.
Just final.

3. The Avoidance Dragon

Shutting down.
Walking away.
Disappearing into their room or their phone.

This dragon loves silent resistance.

Slay it with:

"We'll restart this conversation at 4 PM. Avoiding it doesn't cancel it."

You're not chasing them.
You're anchoring the reality: *we still have to deal with this.*

4. The Power-Grab Dragon

They want the last word, the final say, the whole throne.

This dragon makes your child feel like they run HR, legal, and executive decisions in your house.

Slay it with:

"You can choose A or B. If you don't choose, I'll choose."

You're not crushing their voice — you're containing the chaos.

5. The Escalation Dragon

They go big, loud, and dramatic — hoping you will, too.

This dragon thrives on yelling, slamming, and emotional fireworks.

Slay it with:

"I'll talk when we're both calm. I'll check back in 20 minutes."

You pause the performance.
You don't pause the consequence.

HOW TO SPOT YOUR DRAGON IN 10 SECONDS

When things start spiraling, ask yourself three questions:

What keeps happening over and over again?
(Eye rolls, last-minute chaos, money emergencies, bedtime battles?)

How do I usually respond — and does it actually work?
(Do I yell, over-explain, cave in, rescue, or shut down?)

Who benefits from this pattern staying the same?
(Hint: the dragon. Not you. Not your child.)

If it's predictable, it's a pattern.
If it's a pattern, it's a dragon.
If it's a dragon, it can be named — and slayed.

THE SAFE WORD: "DRAGON"

In our house, we turned "dragon" into a safe word.

Not to avoid consequences —
to avoid collisions.

When a conversation started spiraling, either one of us could say:

"Dragon."

That meant:

We pause the argument.

We don't pause the issue.

We agree to revisit it at a set time.

We refuse to let the pattern win.

We weren't excusing behavior.
We were protecting the relationship.

Because:

A period is a boundary.
"We'll talk at 7 PM." is a boundary.
"We're not raising our voice at each other." is a boundary.

"Dragon" became our reminder:

We slay the pattern.
We do not slay each other.

THE UNIFIED FRONT PROTOCOL (UFP)

The dragon loves division — especially between adults.

It whispers:

"Your spouse is the problem."

"Grandma is the problem."

"You're alone in this."

That's how homes end up with one "strict" parent, one "fun" parent, and a very confused child.

The Unified Front Protocol keeps the dragon from playing you against each other.

Here's the simple version:

Name the Dragon Together
"Our dragon is last-minute chaos before school."
"Our dragon is disrespectful tone in the evenings."

One Clean Sentence
Agree on one clear message you both use.

"No phones at the table."
"No yelling in this house — adults or kids."

One Keepable Consequence
Choose a consequence you can both honor on your tired days.
If it's not keepable, it's not a consequence — it's a speech.

Safe Word for the Adults
Use "Dragon" with each other, too.

"We're getting pulled into the pattern. Let's pause and talk later — just us."

Public Unity, Private Edits
In front of the child, you stand together.
Later, behind closed doors, you can adjust the plan.

TRUTH BOMB for the grown folks:

We disagree in private so our child can grow in public.

The dragon loses power when your home stops being a boxing ring and becomes a team meeting.

THE TRUTH ABOUT YOUR TONE

Here's a hard one:

You can be absolutely right about the issue...
and still be feeding the dragon with your tone.

Volume is panic, not power.

Sarcasm is gasoline, not wisdom.

Repeating yourself fourteen times is fear, not leadership.

Calm is power; volume is panic.

When you lower your voice, you raise your authority.

REFLECT & RESET

REFLECT:
What conflict in my home feels like the same episode on

repeat? What does that dragon look like — backtalk, avoidance, blow-ups, money emergencies, disrespect?

RESET:
What is one short sentence I can start using to name the dragon and separate my child from the pattern? (Example: "We're not fighting each other; we're fighting the pattern.")

LEGACY:
If my child grows up seeing me fight patterns, not people, what will that teach them about marriage, friendship, leadership, and their own future family?

AUDIT

- What dragon shows up most often in my home?
- Do I fight my child instead of the pattern?
- What pattern needs naming so it can finally be broken?

PRAYER

Lord, help me see my child's heart beneath the behavior.
Show me the dragons — the patterns — that keep stealing our peace.
Give me wisdom to fight the right battles,
strength to stay calm,

and courage to stand with my child instead of against them. Amen.

TRUTH BOMB

When you stop fighting your child, the dragon loses every time.

FINAL SAINT LINE

Name the dragon — and suddenly, the battle isn't you versus your child... it's you and your child, standing together on the same side.

CHAPTER FIVE
Respect travels: preparing kids for the real world

Naming the dragon is powerful — but now the real transformation begins.

Once you identify the pattern, you can't just react less... you have to lead better.

You don't need more panic responses.
You need policies.

Chapter Four showed you *what* you're fighting.
Chapter Five shows you *how to win* — with rules, tone, scripts, and daily habits that turn a reactive home into a regulated one.

Because here's the core truth of this chapter:

Respect is not a house rule — it's a life skill.

If your child doesn't learn respect inside your four walls, the world will train them the hard way.

Respect Is a Passport, Not Just a "Please & Thank You"

We treat respect like manners sometimes — cute, optional, something you dust off for company.

But real respect is bigger than that.

Respect:

shapes how your child talks to teachers, coaches, bosses, and partners

decides whether doors swing open… or quietly close

determines if people want to help them or can't wait to be done with them

Home is the training ground.

When your child learns to:

disagree without disrespect

apologize without collapsing

hear "no" without throwing emotional furniture

…they're not just "being good." They're building muscles they will use in classrooms, locker rooms, boardrooms, and courtrooms one day.

Every day at home is a dress rehearsal for how they'll move through the world.

Respect Starts in the Little Things

Respect is woven into everyday life — not just speeches.

It shows up when:

your child waits for everyone to be served before digging in

they knock before entering a room

they borrow a sibling's item and return it the way they found it

they say, "Thank you for dinner," even if it was spaghetti... again

These are not random niceties.
They're reps — repetitions — building character and emotional intelligence.

When you guide your child to:

express frustration without attacking

speak calmly when a sibling crosses a line

listen to a family member's story without interrupting

...you're teaching them how to honor their own
feelings and other people's dignity at the same time.

That's grown-up respect.
We're just training it early.

Boundaries Are Respect in Action

Respect isn't just sweet words. It lives in your boundaries.

When you calmly insist on:

respectful language

no name-calling

no yelling over each other

"we don't slam doors in this house"

...you're sending a clear message:

"How we treat people matters here. Every time."

Boundaries create a safe framework where kids can test limits and still be loved.

They learn:

"I can be mad, but I can't be mean."

"I can disagree, but I can't disrespect."

"I can feel big feelings, but I don't get to burn the whole room down."

Respect is not about making your child small.
It's about teaching them how to be powerful without being harmful.

Respect Travels Further Than You Do

Your child will step into rooms you will never see:

classrooms

Snapchat threads

group chats

job interviews

team huddles

first apartments

You won't be there to whisper, "Fix your tone," or "Say thank you," or "Don't roll your eyes at your boss."

But the training you gave them?
That travels.

Think about the ripple effect:

A child who learns to listen without interrupting at dinner is more likely to listen in class.

A child who learns to own their mistakes at home is more likely to face consequences with humility instead of excuses.

A child who learns to accept "no" at home is less likely to explode when a coach, teacher, or boss sets a limit.

Respect practiced under your roof becomes their
shield and their advantage out in the world.

If You Don't Teach It Gently, the World Will Teach It Harshly

Here's the part we don't like to think about — but we need to.

When respect is missing at home, the world steps in:

A teacher will write them up.

A coach will bench them.

A boss will fire them.

A landlord will evict them.

A police officer will not negotiate with their attitude.

Respect travels because consequences travel.

You have the blessing of teaching it with love, repetition, and grace — before life teaches it with less patience and more cost.

Your home is the safest lab they'll ever have.

They get to mess up, reset, and try again with you.
Out there? The stakes are higher.

Everyday Training Grounds: Where Respect Actually Gets Built

Let's walk through some real-life places where respect is practiced long before adulthood knocks.

Example 1: The Morning Routine — Respecting Time

Your child wakes up late. Again.
Misses the bus. Again.
Walks around like life is a spa day. Again.

Old parenting:

"If you miss that bus one more time! I'm not playing with you!"

Respect-based parenting:

"I leave at 7:15. If you're not ready, you'll need to walk or arrange another ride."

No screaming.
No long speech.

Respect lesson: other people's time matters. The world runs on clocks, not vibes.

Respect grows when consequences exist — and stay consistent.

Example 2: School Interactions — Respecting Authority

Your child storms in:

"My teacher was yelling at me for no reason."

You start asking questions, and the truth comes out in fragments:

"I mean, I was talking but not that much..."

"She told me to stop..."

"I just said she was being dramatic..."

There it is.

Respect lesson:

"You can disagree. But *how* and *when* you disagree determines the outcome. Let's practice a better response."

No shame.
No "You embarrassed me at that school."

Just clarity and rehearsal.

You're not raising a robot who agrees with everyone.
You're raising a child who can speak up without setting their own future on fire.

Example 3: Home Chores — Respecting Shared Space

Your child leaves dishes in the sink like an invisible maid lives there.

Old you:

"I'm so tired of cleaning up after everybody in this house!"

Respect-based you:

"Dishes are to be washed by 8 PM. If they're still in the sink after that, kitchen privileges pause until they're done."

Respect lesson:
Shared space = shared responsibility.

It's not punishment.
It's preparation for roommates, spouses, and future landlords who will not care about their feelings when the sink is full.

Example 4: Speaking to Adults — Respecting Tone

A child who responds with "What?" instead of "Ma'am?" or "What?" instead of "Sir?"
is practicing a tone that will cost them opportunities later.

You train tone with simple scripts:

"Try that again."

"Say that respectfully."

"Use your indoor voice."

"You can be honest without being rude."

You're not nitpicking.
You're protecting their future.

The world does not accept disrespect wrapped in adolescence.

Your training will cover them in rooms where your name is never mentioned.

Example 5: Phones & Tech — Respecting Boundaries

Screens are the new battleground.

Your child slams their door and announces:

"I'm grown!"

...while still using your Wi-Fi, eating your food, and living at your address.

Respect-based response:

"When your tone drops, your privileges pause. We'll reset when respect returns."

Not spite.
Not revenge.

Just a clear connection between behavior and access.

Technology becomes a monster only when it outranks the parent.

Respect Is Not Fear — It's Preparation

Let's be clear:

Respect is not your child being scared of you.
Respect is your child understanding:

"My words matter."

"My tone matters."

"Other people's boundaries matter."

"The way I show up affects my opportunities."

Kids who learn respect are:

easier to teach

easier to coach

easier to employ

easier to love

safer in adulthood

Respect is a life jacket.
You are fastening the straps before the ocean gets deep.

Modeling: The Respect They See Becomes the Respect They Give

You can't demand what you don't demonstrate.

Your child watches:

how you talk to waitstaff

how you talk about teachers behind their backs

how you treat the neighbor who gets on your nerves

how you handle being wrong

how you talk to *them* when you're tired

If you yell at everyone then say, "But you better not talk like that"?
That's confusion, not training.

But when they see you:

listen without interrupting

apologize when you blow it

say "thank you" like you mean it

cool off before responding in anger

...they absorb those behaviors as normal.

You're not just teaching respect; you're normalizing it.

Make Respect a Muscle, Not a Moment

Respect isn't learned in one lecture after they mess up.

It's built like a muscle:

through repetition

through practice

through feedback

through do-overs

Some practical ways to build the muscle:

Invite them to share opinions in family meetings — respectfully.

Let them help resolve sibling disagreements — with guidance.

Role-play hard conversations — with teachers, coaches, friends.

Talk after family gatherings:
"Did you hear how Uncle handled that disagreement? What did you notice?"

These aren't grand performances.
They're small reps that become big habits.

REFLECT & RESET

REFLECT:
Where do I see respect slipping most — tone, chores, school, tech, sibling interactions?

RESET:
What is one small respect expectation I will clarify and enforce this week — with calm, not shame? (Example: "No phones at the table," or "We don't shout from room to room.")

LEGACY:
If my child learns to carry respect into classrooms, jobs, and relationships, what kind of doors will that open for them that my generation had to learn the hard way?

AUDIT

- Where is respect slipping in my home?
- Am I teaching it... or tolerating the lack of it?

- What consequence can reinforce respect without harshness — clear, consistent, and calm?

PRAYER

Lord, teach me to model the respect I expect.
Help me guide my child with firmness and kindness.
Give me wisdom to correct without shaming,
and strength to stay consistent when I'm tired.
Shape their character through our daily choices,
and let respect become their covering wherever they go.
Amen.

TRUTH BOMB

Respect at home becomes safety everywhere else.

FINAL SAINT LINE

Train respect now — so the world doesn't have to do it later.

CHAPTER SIX
The safe word protocol: pausing the storm without losing control

The first time my daughter and I used a safe word, it felt awkward — like we were following a script somebody forgot to explain.

We were sitting at the kitchen table, tension humming in the air.
We weren't yelling yet, but we were close.

I could see it in her eyes.
She could hear it in my voice.

"This feels a little strange," I admitted. "But I want us to try something new."

She looked at me — skeptical but listening.

"A safe word?" she asked. "Like a movie?"

"Kind of," I said. "It's just a word we both agree on. When either of us says it, we pause the conversation — not the consequences — and come back when we're calmer."

It wasn't smooth.
It wasn't magical.

We laughed nervously.
We practiced the word a couple of times and felt silly.

But underneath the awkwardness, something important was happening:

We were building a shared tool.

We were saying, "Our relationship matters more than winning the argument."

We were giving ourselves permission to pause before we burned the whole house down over one moment.

That's what the Safe Word Protocol really is:

Not a trick.
Not a loophole.
Not a way to dodge hard conversations.

It's a pause button that protects both the boundary and the relationship.

Why We Needed a Safe Word

Before we created our protocol, our conflicts followed the same tired script:

She'd raise her voice.

I'd raise mine just a little higher.

She'd get sharp.

I'd get triggered.

We'd both say too much, too fast, too loud.

Nobody felt heard.
Nobody felt safe.
And nothing truly changed — except the distance between us.

I realized something had to give.

I didn't want a home where every boundary conversation felt like a courtroom or a battlefield. I wanted a way to teach respect and model emotional regulation at the same time.

I didn't just want fewer arguments.
I wanted better arguments.

So we tried something new.

Building the Safe Word Together

I didn't announce the protocol like a royal decree from the stairs.

We built it together.

One calm afternoon, I said:

"Sometimes our feelings run faster than our words. I don't want us to say things we can't take back. I'd like us to have a safe word — something either of us can say when we need a pause."

We talked honestly about what we both needed in those moments:

She wanted space without feeling punished.

I wanted respect without feeling attacked.

We both wanted to be heard without every disagreement turning into a shouting match.

Then we picked a word.

You can choose any neutral, harmless word. Some families use colors. Some use something silly to break the tension. Some, like we talk about in this book, even use "Dragon" — because it reminds everyone the pattern is the problem, not the person.

In our protocol, we chose:

"Dragon."

"Dragon" meant:

Emotions are rising.

We're about to cross a line.

We need a pause, not a punishment.

We practiced it once or twice during a calm moment so it wouldn't feel foreign when we actually needed it.

It felt awkward.
But it also felt hopeful.

We weren't just reacting anymore.
We were planning.

The Day "Dragon" Went Live

She was seventeen, and we were arguing about curfew.

Her tone was getting sharp.
My patience was thinning.

Old patterns were rising fast.

I could feel my chest tighten — not just from the moment, but from every other argument we'd ever had about responsibility, respect, and whose rules mattered.

Then she said it:

"Dragon."

Everything froze.

Not because the word had magic…
but because it had agreement.

We had already decided what "Dragon" meant:

"Dragon" means pause, not stop.

"Dragon" means emotion is high.

"Dragon" means we step away and return in 20 minutes.

"Dragon" does not cancel consequences.

"I hear you," I said. "Dragon. We'll pause and talk in 20 minutes."

I walked to my room.
She went to hers.

No slamming.
No shouting.
No "You always…" or "You never…"

Twenty minutes later, we met in the living room.

We weren't perfect.
But we were calmer.

We could actually listen.

The curfew consequence stayed.
The rule didn't change.

But the way we handled it did.

The Safe Word Protocol didn't just save that night.
It started saving our relationship.

Why Safe Words Work

Safe words give structure during emotional storms.

They teach your child:

Feelings aren't emergencies.

Pausing isn't quitting.

You can step away without losing control.

Consequences still stand, even when emotions pause.

Conflict can be revisited calmly — not avoided forever.

This is emotional intelligence training in real time.

You are quietly teaching your child:

"Big feelings are allowed.
Big disrespect is not.
We can feel everything — and still keep the standard."

You're not just avoiding blow-ups.
You're modeling what regulated leadership looks like.

The Safe Word Protocol (Step-by-Step)

Here's a simple way to build this in your home.

1. Choose the Word Together

Pick something neutral and easy:

A color: Yellow, Blue, Orange

A random word: Pineapple, Library, Pause

A symbolic word: Dragon (for "fight the pattern, not the person")

The word doesn't carry the power.
The agreement does.

2. Explain What It Means

Use plain language:

"When someone says the safe word, we stop talking for a set time. That pause is for calming down — not for running away. Consequences still stand. We will return to the conversation."

No mystery.
No tricks.

Just a clear, shared rule.

3. Set a Clear Time Frame

For younger kids: 10–15 minutes.

For teens: 20–30 minutes.

For adult kids: agree on a specific time —

"Let's pick this up at 6 PM."

No silent treatment.
No ghosting.
No "we'll see."

The pause has a clock, not a grudge.

4. Set Behavior Rules During the Pause

The pause is for regulation, not performance.

During a "Dragon" pause:

No yelling from the other room.

No sending 47 angry texts.

No slamming cabinets and calling it "just cleaning."

No posting about it online.

You can say:

"This break is for calming down, not for adding fuel. We'll both take a breath, then come back and finish this."

5. Always Come Back

If you say you'll resume at 6:00, show up at 6:00.

Even if the conversation is brief:

"We're calmer now. Here's the consequence. Here's why. I still love you. We can move forward."

Your credibility lives in the follow-through.

A safe word without follow-through becomes another broken promise — and the dragon loves broken promises.

Real-Life Examples: Safe Word in Action

Example 1: The Teen Tantrum

They're yelling.
You're annoyed.
Both of you are seconds away from saying something nuclear.

You:

"Dragon. We pause. Back in 15 minutes."

Then — and this is the important part — you actually walk away.

No muttering.
No "Let me say one last thing…"
No mini-sermon in the hallway.

Just pause.

The atmosphere resets.

Example 2: The Parent Trigger

Sometimes you are the one who needs the safe word.

Your child's tone hits an old wound. Suddenly, you're not just a parent — you're the hurt kid you used to be.

You:

"Dragon for me. I need a moment."

Then you model the grown-up move:

Step away.

Breathe.

Pray.

Return calmer.

That is not weakness.
That is leadership.

You are teaching your child:

"Even adults need tools. Pausing is wisdom, not failure."

Example 3: The Adult Child Argument

Adult kids argue like lawyers with feelings.

You're going back and forth about:

money

visits

boundaries

choices

relationships

...and you feel yourself getting flooded.

You:

"Dragon. We're escalating. Let's resume this at 6 PM."

You're not shutting them down.
You're protecting the relationship.

You are saying:

"We can disagree without destroying what we have."

The Safe Word Protocol grows with your family — from toddlers to twenty-somethings.

Guardrails: What the Safe Word Is *Not*

The safe word is powerful — but only if it has boundaries.

It is NOT:

an escape hatch

a loophole

a way to avoid consequences

a magic spell that erases the rule

a shutdown button your child can hit anytime they don't like your answer

It is simply:

A cooling-off timer.

The boundary stays.
The tone changes.

You can say:

"Dragon pauses the conversation, not the consequence."

"We'll still address what happened after the break."

"You can use the safe word to cool down, not to dodge accountability."

If your child starts abusing the safe word — saying it every time they're asked to do anything — you tighten the policy:

"You can use 'Dragon' when emotions are high.
You cannot use it to avoid instructions. If you misuse it, I'll finish the direction first and then we can call 'Dragon.'"

Remember:

This tool is for regulation, not manipulation.

Script Library: How to Actually Say It

Here are a few lines you can borrow and adapt:

"I hear you're upset. I'm calling 'Dragon.' We'll come back to this in 20 minutes."

"You just used our safe word — good choice. Let's go to separate rooms and calm down."

"'Dragon' pauses the conversation, not the consequence. The rule still stands."

"I love you. We'll finish this when both our voices are calmer."

"I'm not walking away from *you*. I'm walking away from the argument so we don't say things we regret."

These phrases teach your child that pausing is not abandonment — it's protection.

Why This Matters for Emotional Safety

Using a safe word consistently teaches your child:

You can be upset and still be safe.

Conflict does not automatically mean disconnection.

Boundaries can be firm and kind.

Feelings are signals, not dictators.

Pausing is a strength, not a weakness.

You're not just avoiding blow-ups.
You're building your child's emotional toolkit.

You're teaching a skill they will need with:

spouses

bosses

friends

roommates

their own future children

The Safe Word Protocol is not about making your home "nice."
It's about making your home safe — emotionally, spiritually, and relationally.

REFLECT & RESET

REFLECT:
When conflict rises in our home, do we escalate, avoid, or actually resolve? What patterns keep replaying the same way?

RESET:
What word could our family agree on as a safe word — and when will I introduce it calmly, not in the middle of a fight?

LEGACY:
If my child grows up knowing how to pause, breathe, and come back to hard conversations with respect, how will that

change their marriage, their parenting, and their leadership one day?

AUDIT

- What word will our home use to pause conflict?
- Do I model emotional regulation — or do I escalate right alongside my child?
- How quickly do I return to calm after conflict, and what needs to change?

PRAYER

Lord, help me lead with calm when emotions rise.
Teach me to pause instead of exploding.
Give me the wisdom to step back before I say what I can't unsay,
and the courage to come back and finish hard conversations with love and clarity.
Let peace guide my words and wisdom guide my timing.
Amen.

TRUTH BOMB

A pause isn't surrender — it's strategy

FINAL SAINT LINE

Pause the storm, not the standard.

CHAPTER SEVEN
The money boundary: teaching contribution, not chaos

The Saturday Morning Cash-App Ambush

It always starts the same way.

Saturday morning.
You're minding your business, sipping coffee, scrolling your peace.

Then — ding.

Your phone lights up with the most predictable message in modern parenting:

"Can you Cash App me $20 real quick?"

And the follow-up, five minutes later:

"Did you send it?"

No greeting.
No context.
Just entitlement with Wi-Fi.

That's the moment most parents slide into the same tired cycle:

Request → Pressure → Parent caves → Child learns nothing.

Every time you hit *Send* just to "keep the peace," what you're really funding is a cycle of dependency.

Because here's the truth:

Money problems are rarely about money.
They are boundary problems wearing dollar-sign disguises.

Children who treat your wallet like a vending machine don't magically grow into adults who value contribution.
They grow into adults who expect rescue.

But when you shift the script and calmly respond with:

"What's the plan?
What's the need?
And what's your contribution?"

...everything changes.

You send three silent messages that will follow them into adulthood:

Money is earned, not extracted.

Support has structure.

You are not being raised to depend — you are being raised to contribute.

This chapter is about helping your child step out of chaos and into responsibility — not through lectures, not through yelling, but through clear money boundaries that teach life skills, not stress.

Let's walk this out, one real-life moment at a time.

Why Money Exposes Everything

Money reveals patterns faster than any chore chart, grounding rule, or family meeting.

A child who avoids chores will avoid contribution.

A child who pressures you for spending money will pressure partners, bosses, and friends later.

A child who gets rewarded for attitude learns that manipulation pays.

Money doesn't create the pattern.
It magnifies what's already there.

Your job isn't to fund the pattern — it's to interrupt it.

When you:

pause before giving,

ask questions before transferring,

require contribution before compensation...

...you shift your home from:

Chaos → Clarity
Entitlement → Effort
Rescue → Responsibility

REAL-LIFE MONEY MOMENTS

These scenarios show exactly where boundaries build maturity.

Example 1: The "Will-You-Cash-App-Me" Cycle

Child:

"Can you Cash App me $20 real quick?"

Old you: *sigh*

"Fine..."

You send it. You feel used. They learn nothing.

New you:

"What's the plan, what's the need, and what's your contribution?"

You are calmly saying:

Money is a conversation, not a reflex.

You don't fund fog. You fund plans.

This one-line alone cuts entitlement in half.

If they can't clearly answer those three questions, the answer is simple:

"Looks like this isn't a today request. Try again when you have a plan."

Example 2: The Chore-Chaos Pattern

They want:

Wi-Fi

Rides

Outings

Food that didn't come from your Tupperware

...but treat chores like they're allergic.

New policy:

"Privileges follow contribution."

Not punishment — preparation.

You're teaching:

"In this house, everyone eats, everyone messes, everyone contributes."

"Comfort is connected to responsibility, not just to asking nicely."

You don't have to yell:

"When the bathroom is cleaned by 6 PM, the Wi-Fi returns. Not before."

Household standards become a money language.

Example 3: The Borrowing Loop

They borrow your:

chargers

headphones

clothes

car

...and somehow everything comes back missing, broken, or "I don't know what happened."

New boundary:

"If you lose what you borrow, you reimburse it."

No speech.
No dragging it out.

Just:

"You lost it. The replacement costs $25. Let's talk about how you're going to pay it back."

Natural consequence = accountability.

You're not being petty. You're teaching:

"What doesn't belong to you deserves respect."

"Carelessness has a cost."

Example 4: The Teen Job Reset

Teens don't need a full-time job to become responsible — but they absolutely need skin in the game.

Starter budget options:

Phone bill: they contribute $10–$25 each month.

Gas: they pay a portion or fill the tank twice a month.

Outings: they use allowance or job money, not just your card.

This teaches:

value

planning

self-control

responsibility

You're shifting the mindset from:

"Mom will figure it out."

to

"Let me figure out my part."

Money becomes a mirror showing how ready they are for adult life.

Example 5: The Parent Guilt Cycle

They look stressed.
They make a sad face.
They tell you all their friends have it.

Your chest tightens.
Your guilt flares.
Your card comes out.

You buy, rescue, and overgive.

But guilt spending teaches one lesson:

"Apply emotional pressure, and money appears."

You're not teaching love.
You're teaching leverage.

Reset it with:

"Love is free. Money is earned."

You can say:

"I'm always here emotionally.
Money, though, is based on plans, budget, and contribution."

You're separating support from subsidizing chaos.

WHY FINANCIAL BOUNDARIES WORK

When kids learn how to:

contribute,

save,

respect limits,

earn trust,

delay gratification...

...they walk into adulthood prepared, not panicked.

Financial boundaries build:

independence – "I can figure it out."

respect – "Their time and resources matter."

responsibility – "My choices have outcomes."

gratitude – "Help is a gift, not a guarantee."

decision-making – "I can choose where my money goes."

planning – "I need a plan before I ask."

And yes — they build peace.

Because nothing drains a parent faster than financial chaos inside their own home.

Boundaries restore peace and prepare your child for real-world expectations.

REFLECT & RESET

REFLECT:
Where am I feeling the most money stress with my child — constant small asks, big emergencies, broken items, or unpaid responsibilities?

RESET:
What is one sentence I can start using this week to shift the tone?

(Example: "What's the plan, the need, and your contribution?" or "Love is free; money is earned.")

LEGACY:
If my child learns now that money requires planning, effort, and respect, how will that protect them in college, relationships, and future jobs?

AUDIT

Ask yourself:

Where is money fueling stress in my home?

Am I rescuing... or requiring?

What is one financial boundary I can introduce today — calmly and clearly?

PRAYER

Lord, help me guide my child toward responsibility.
Give me the courage to stop rescuing and start preparing.
Teach me to lead with love, firmness, and wisdom in every money decision.
Show me how to model stewardship, not fear.
Amen.

TRUTH BOMB

When you stop rescuing, your child starts rising.

FINAL SAINT LINE

Require contribution, and entitlement has nowhere to grow.

CHAPTER EIGHT
When grown kids test your peace

There is a moment in every parent's life when your child becomes grown...
but not grown-up.

They've got car keys, a bank card, maybe a lease or a job — but emotionally?
You still hear the same old patterns: excuses, emergencies, "Can you fix it?"

That moment will test your peace like nothing you've experienced before.

Because now the stakes are higher.
The bills are bigger.
The consequences are real.

And the question quietly sitting in your chest is this:

"Do I keep rescuing...
or do I finally let them rise?"

The Liminal Space: Grown but Not Grown-Up

Parenting little ones is physical.
Parenting teens is emotional.
Parenting grown kids?

That's spiritual warfare with your calendar and your Cash App.

You stand in a strange hallway:

You're not changing diapers.

You're not signing permission slips.

You're not calling teachers.

But the phone still rings.
The texts still come.
The asks are bigger.

And each request becomes a test — not just of their maturity, but of your willingness to let go.

I had night after night of staring at the ceiling, wondering:

"If I say no, will she think I don't love her?"

"Did I fail her if she's still struggling like this?"

"Am I being harsh... or finally being honest?"

I realized my urge to rescue wasn't just about love.
It was about fear:

Fear that she might fail.

Fear that I hadn't prepared her enough.

Fear that if I didn't step in, everything would fall apart.

One night, in that quiet tug-of-war between my heart and my head, I finally told myself the truth:

"Peace won't come from solving everything for her.
Peace will come from trusting what I already put in her."

That's the doorway every parent of a grown child eventually stands in:

Do I swoop in and shield them from the fallout of their choices,
or do I let them feel the weight of responsibility and discover their strength?

The Internal Battle No One Sees

Grown-kid parenting is full of invisible battles:

On the outside, you're just sitting on the couch.
On the inside, you're wrestling a whole storm.

One part of you wants to rescue.

One part of you wants to scream.

One part of you wants to block the number and take a nap.

And in the middle of those parts is the parent who loves deeply and is tired of being the emergency contact for problems you did not create.

I had to remind myself:

Loving her didn't mean cushioning every fall.

Protecting her didn't mean paying for every mistake.

Supporting her didn't mean sacrificing my peace or my retirement.

It is a bittersweet rite of passage — the day you decide:

"I will not keep paying for decisions I didn't make."

The ache you feel when you step back doesn't mean you stopped loving your child.
It means you started loving them with a long-term vision, not just short-term relief.

When the Theory Meets the Phone Call

It's easy to talk big about boundaries in your head.
It's different when your phone actually rings.

All my "one day I'm going to stop rescuing" speeches ran smack into real life…
over a parking ticket.

My daughter was twenty.

Old enough to drive.
Old enough to vote.
Old enough, in her mind, to make grown decisions...

...but apparently not old enough to pay a $95 ticket she earned by ignoring a "No Parking" sign.

She called me, voice urgent — but not humble urgent. Entitled urgent.

"Mom, I need $95 real quick because the city is trippin'."

No hello.
No "How are you?"
No ownership.

Just:

"Give me the money."

And I'll be honest with you:
My old self woke up immediately.

The fixer.
The rescuer.
The woman who would bend herself into a pretzel to keep her child from feeling discomfort.

My brain was already mapping how to send the money.
"Maybe I can move this bill... pay that later... it's only $95..."

But something in me — the healed version, the calm spine version — rose up and said:

"Hold on, Dee."

So instead of opening my banking app,
I took a breath
and asked one simple question:

"Why is this my emergency?"

Silence.

She tried again, tone shifting now:

"Well… you know I'm trying… and things are stressful… and—"

I cut in — not harsh, but firm.

"I love you.
But love is not a substitute for responsibility.
You created this problem.
You will solve this problem."

My heart was pounding.
My thumb was itching to hit Send anyway.

But instead of caving, I gave her a boundary with a clock:

"You have 30 days to get a job or enroll in school.
If not, the car comes back home."

No yelling.
No three-hour sermon.
No dramatic exit.

Just clarity.

She was furious.

She hung up.
She sent paragraphs that read like a whole dissertation in manipulation.
I won't lie — the guilt tried to choke me.

But I stayed calm.

Not because I didn't care —
because I cared enough to stop raising a gray-haired toddler.

And in 10 days…

She got a job.

No Cash App.
No rescue.
No bailout.

Just a grown decision from a grown kid
who finally realized Mom wasn't the bank anymore.

That day taught me something I'll never forget:

Grown kids aren't really testing your money.
They're testing your leadership.

Why Grown Kids Push Harder

Adult children push harder for a reason:

The bills are bigger.

The consequences are real.

And they've had years of watching what you'll do under pressure.

They know:

Your soft spots.

Your guilt buttons.

Your history of "just this once."

They want adult privileges with child benefits.

And because you love them, your heart wants to believe:

"This time is different.
This time it really is an emergency.
This time, if I help, they'll change."

But patterns don't change because you pay them.
Patterns change because you stop funding them.

Here's the truth:

Even adult children still need boundaries.

They actually respect you more when you set them.

Your "no" doesn't break the relationship — it clarifies it.

The Three Types of Grown-Kid Pressure

Most grown-kid drama lands in one of three categories.

1. Emotional Pressure

"I'm stressed!"
"You don't understand!"
"You're making this worse!"

They throw feelings like invoices.

Reality check:
Emotion is not a bill you have to pay.

You can say:

"I hear you're stressed.
I'm still not sending money.
Let's talk about your plan instead."

2. Crisis Pressure

Everything is an emergency.

"They're gonna cut it off TODAY."
"If I don't pay by tonight, it's over."
"You have to help me RIGHT NOW."

Adult kids are famous for manufacturing urgency out of problems they ignored for weeks.

Crisis language doesn't mean you have to move.

You can respond:

"I'm sorry it's urgent.
I will not be funding this.
What are *your* options?"

3. Guilt Pressure

"You're my mom."
"You're supposed to help."
"You did it before."

The subtext is:

"If you loved me, you'd fix it."

But guilt is not a valid reason to break your own boundaries.

Repeat after me:

Guilt is not guidance.

You can love your child and say:

"I love you deeply.
And I will not be paying for this."

What Your Peace Teaches Your Adult Child

Your peace is a whole sermon.

Your peace quietly says:

"Your chaos doesn't control me."

"Your urgency is not my responsibility."

"Your choices belong to you."

"I love you — but I will not carry you."

You don't have to slam doors, block numbers, or give cold shoulders.

Calm, steady peace is a form of leadership grown children understand — even if they pretend, they don't.

Because when you stop panicking:

They can't use crisis to move you.

They can't use tears to trap you.

They can't use guilt to guide you.

Your peace becomes the moment they realize:

"If I want a different outcome... I have to make a different choice."

How to Hold the Line Without Losing the Relationship

Here's a simple rhythm you can follow when a grown child is pushing your boundaries:

Validate the feeling.

"I hear that you're frustrated."

"I can tell this is stressing you out."

State the boundary.

"But I will not be paying for this."

"I'm not taking this on as my emergency."

Redirect the responsibility.

"What's your plan?"

"How are you going to handle this?"

Hold the silence.
Let the pause work on them.
Don't rush to fill it with solutions.

Reconnect calmly.

"I believe in your ability to figure this out."

"I am confident in your ability to work this through."

This rhythm does not make you cold.
It makes you clear.

And clarity is what turns:

emotional childhood into

emotional adulthood.

Scripts for When Your Grown Kid Tests Your Peace

Use these lines as training wheels while you find your voice:

"I love you. I'm not transferring money."

"I'm available for brainstorming, not bailouts."

"I'm not raising a gray-haired toddler."

"I'm not the solution — you are."

"I'm willing to help with a *plan*, not a panic."

"We don't fund the same mistake twice."

Tiny sentences.

Big shift.

REFLECT & RESET

REFLECT:

Where am I stepping in for my grown child in ways that keep them from feeling the weight of their own choices?

RESET:

What is one clear money or rescue boundary I can communicate this week — calmly and without a long speech?

LEGACY:

If my grown child learns now that "My life is my responsibility," how will that change their future — jobs, relationships, and their own children?

AUDIT

Where am I rescuing a grown child who should be rescuing themselves?

What pattern with my adult child needs breaking *today* — repeated bailouts, emotional emergencies, last-minute panics?

What boundary have I avoided because I'm afraid of their reaction... and what will it cost us if I never set it?

PRAYER

Lord, help me lead my grown child with love and wisdom.
Give me courage to hold boundaries even when emotions rise.
Remind me that my job is to prepare, not to rescue forever.
Let my peace teach them what my panic never could.
Help them see their own strength, and help me trust the foundation we've built.
Amen.

TRUTH BOMB

A grown child will test your peace to see if you still remember your power.

FINAL SAINT LINE

When you step back, they step up.

CHAPTER NINE
No cash, just clarity: the annual loan rule

I tell parents everywhere:

"I only loan money once a year."

It sounds funny — but baby, it works.

Because grown kids will turn your generosity into
a subscription service if you let them.
Auto-draft.
On-demand.
No login required.

And listen — this rule isn't stingy.
It isn't petty.
It isn't punishment.

It's leadership.

It's the moment you stand up in your own home and say:

"I love you too much to keep financing your chaos."

The Annual Loan Rule does three powerful things at once:

It forces planning.

It forces accountability.

It forces grown kids to stop acting like you're Wells Fargo with soft lighting and warm cookies.

But most importantly, it puts you back in control of your peace.

Why This Rule Changes Everything

Money is emotional.
Money is power.
Money is patterns.

If you don't put structure around it, the money in your home will run you ragged.

The Annual Loan Rule breaks all three dysfunctional cycles at once.

When your child knows they only get ONE financial rescue per year, everything shifts:

They plan better.

They save more.

They stop turning your love into a panic button.

They start respecting your boundaries because now they're predictable.

This rule teaches:

"My love is unconditional, but my money is not."

And once you master that sentence — whew — your whole house shifts.

How It Works (Real Life, Not Theory)

Let's walk through how this rule actually plays out in real homes, with real grown kids, and real parents who were tired of being everybody's bailout plan.

The Big Ask — The Day It All Changed

A mother I coached had a 23-year-old son who "borrowed" money every month.

By the time she found me, she had paid for:

Rent

Car repairs

"Emergencies"

Grocery money

Gaming money disguised as groceries

A phone bill she didn't even know existed

She felt drained.
He felt entitled.

I gave her the Annual Loan Rule.

She swallowed hard — but she meant it.

The next month he texted:

"I need $120 real quick."

Old her would've sighed, complained to a friend, then sent it anyway.

New her typed:

"You already used your annual loan in February."

Silence.
Then attitude.
Then shock.
Then... responsibility.

He picked up a second job.

Not because she nagged.
Not because she yelled.
Not because she gave a three-hour lecture on adulthood.

Because boundaries create clarity — and clarity creates adulthood.

Scenario 1: The Car Breakdown

Your child calls frantic:

"Mom, my tire blew! I need money now!"

Old pattern:
You send it immediately because you don't want them stranded — and secretly you're afraid to see them struggle.

New pattern:

"I'll help *one* time this year. This is it. After today, you'll need to build an emergency fund."

You help.
Once.

And you tie it to a principle:
"Car owners plan ahead. This is your wake-up call."

They learn: Preparation beats panic.

Scenario 2: The Rent Shortage

They made choices instead of payments.
Nails, trips, DoorDash, outfits — all of it felt urgent until rent showed up looking for its money.

They call, panicked.

Old you:

"Okay, I'll help... but this is the last time."
(You both know that's a lie.)

New you:

"This will count as your annual loan. I'll help this month. What's your plan for next month?"

You're not just wiring money — you're forcing them to think past today.

They learn: Budgeting is grown-up math.

Scenario 3: The Habitual Borrower

For them, your wallet is a revolving door. They "borrow" like it's a personality trait.

New message:

"You get one loan annually. You already used it. I believe in your ability to figure it out."

That's it. No extra speech.

They may pout.
They may flip it back on you.
They may send guilt-laced paragraphs.

But the rule stands.

They learn:
Problem-solving is their job, not yours.

Scenario 4: The Guilt Trip

You finally say no.

They respond with:

"Oh wow... I see what kind of mom you are."
"You don't care about me."
"You helped me before — why not now?"

And baby — NOPE.

You breathe, then calmly respond:

"I love you.
And I'm done financing chaos."

Then you let the silence do the teaching.

You're not mean.
You're not cold.
You're just not available for the same pattern anymore.

The Bonus Rule: No Cash. Ever.

Here's where the rule gets even stronger:

Never transfer cash.

Not Cash App.
Not Zelle.
Not "just this one time."

If you choose to help, you pay the vendor, never the child.

Because accountability grows when the money trail is clean.

Tires → paid to the tire shop.

Clinic → paid to the clinic.

School → paid to the school.

Cash disappears.
Receipts don't.

This one shift exposes the truth fast:

Real needs stay.

Fake emergencies evaporate.

Why This Rule Works (The Psychology Behind It)

The Annual Loan Rule works because it removes you from the emotional tornado.

You are no longer:

The bad guy

The ATM

The bailout

The negotiator

The guilt sponge

The emotional punching bag

You become something much more powerful:

You are policy.

And grown kids don't argue with policy —
they eventually adapt to it.

Once the rule is clear:

They stop calling every crisis "once in a lifetime."

They start thinking before swiping.

They start building their own safety nets.

They may not like it at first.
But they will grow because of it.

The Beauty of Clear Boundaries

When you say:

"Love is free. Money is earned."

You're not rejecting your child —
you're revealing their strength.

You're saying:

"I believe you're capable."

"I trust you to figure it out."

"I will not carry what belongs to you."

Over time, your child becomes:

More creative

More resourceful

More mature

More grounded

More aware of consequences

More grateful when help actually comes

This rule teaches adulthood, not dependence.

And your peace?
It skyrockets.

Your savings account exhales.
Your nervous system calms down.

Your "no" starts working harder than your overdraft line ever did.

REFLECT & RESET

REFLECT:
Where have I been using my bank account to manage my child's emotions instead of my own boundaries?

RESET:
If I adopted the Annual Loan Rule, what needs to change — today — about how and when I send money?

LEGACY:
What kind of adult will my child become if they learn *now* that support has structure, and love doesn't always come with a transfer?

AUDIT

Do I give money to my child more than once a year?

Do I send cash without clarity, receipts, or a written plan?

Where is my child depending on me instead of maturing?

PRAYER

Lord, give me wisdom in how I support my child financially.
Help me teach maturity instead of enabling irresponsibility.
Give me the courage to hold money boundaries with love, not anger.
Let my "no" protect both my peace and their future.
Amen.

TRUTH BOMB

A boundary around money is a boundary around your peace.

FINAL SAINT LINE

Clarity teaches what cash never will.

CHAPTER TEN
Reclaiming your crown: parenting without over-functioning

There comes a day in almost every parent's life when you stop in the middle of your own house and think:

"I am doing way too much... for people who are doing way too little."

For me, it was a Wednesday.

Not a holiday. Not a crisis. Just one of those regular, relentless days where the dishwasher was full, the laundry pile looked like a mountain range, and every child in the house needed something from me except oxygen.

I was moving on autopilot—loading, folding, wiping, answering, finding, fixing—while everyone else floated through the house like guests at an all-inclusive resort. They were laughing in the next room, asking what was for dinner, stepping over backpacks and trash like they lived in a museum instead of a home.

And something in me whispered:

"This is not sustainable."

At first it felt like ordinary tired. But under that regular tired was something deeper—a bone-deep ache that said, *You're carrying more than your share*. Every time I stepped in to rescue, pick up, remind, or rearrange, a little bit of me faded into the background.

I wasn't just doing the work.
I was disappearing inside the work.

When Love Starts to Hurt

If you're like me, you didn't get here because you don't love your kids. You got here because you love them a lot.

You wanted to be the safe place. The steady one. The person who could be counted on when everything else fell apart. So when life got messy, you did what loving parents do—you stepped in.

You tied the shoes.
You finished the projects.
You drove across town with the forgotten gym bag.
You stayed up late to fix what they ignored all day.

At first, it feels like love. And it *is* love. But slowly, something shifts.

The more you do, the more everyone expects you to do.
The more you anticipate their needs, the less anyone notices yours.
The more you smooth every rough edge, the fewer edges anybody else ever has to grow over.

One Wednesday, standing in my kitchen surrounded by crumbs, dishes, and voices calling "Mom!" from three directions, I felt a wave of loneliness I couldn't ignore. It wasn't just that I was tired—I felt invisible.

It hit me:

I had created a system where everyone else got to grow, rest, and lean...
and I was the only one holding up the whole house.

That's when another truth rose up in my spirit, clear and calm:

"You have been over-functioning in a house full of people who are perfectly capable of learning how to function too."

Over-Functioning: The Exhausting Illusion

Over-functioning is when you consistently do for others what they are capable of doing, learning, or at least *attempting* for themselves.

It sounds like:

"It's faster if I just do it."

"They've had a long day; I'll pick up the slack."

"At least this way it gets done right."

"I don't want the argument, so I'll handle it."

And underneath all of that?

A quiet fear:

If I don't hold everything together, everything will fall apart.

So you carry their responsibilities, their feelings, their consequences, and sometimes even their relationship with God—on your back. You call it love, but it's really a kind of control. A scared, exhausted, well-intentioned control that says:

"If I hurt, they don't have to."

But here's the part nobody tells you:

Every time you stand in the gap they were supposed to grow across,
you are teaching them that your time is cheaper than their effort.

You don't mean to.
You're not trying to raise entitled kids.

But over-functioning is how entitlement quietly grows in a home that's full of love.

When Your Reflection Tells the Truth

One night, I was in the laundry room folding towels like it was a full-time ministry. The house was buzzing, my body was on automatic, but my soul was just... tired.

I caught my reflection in the shiny door of the washing machine. Same face. Same eyes. But there was a worn look I couldn't excuse away anymore. I thought about my own mother—how she did it all, how I rarely saw her rest, how her love looked like constant motion.

And then it hit me:

I am teaching my kids the exact same thing I told myself I would never repeat:
that a mother's love means disappearing inside everybody else's needs.

I knew I wanted a different legacy.

Not a legacy of a mom who "did it all,"
but a mom who loved well and lived.

A mom whose kids knew how to cook, clean, plan, recover, repair, apologize, and contribute—because she *let* them.
A mom who didn't just preach boundaries, but modeled them.

Right there, surrounded by laundry, I knew something had to change.

The Moment the Crown Slipped Back On

Fast forward to that Wednesday in the kitchen.

The trash was overflowing.
A backpack was on the floor like modern art.
Dishes were stacked.
I hadn't sat down in what felt like three hours.

My daughter walked into the kitchen, opened the fridge, and—with full confidence—asked:

"Mom, what's for dinner?"

Something in my spirit stood up before my body did.

"Oh... absolutely not."

Not in anger.
Not in bitterness.

In clarity.

In that moment, I could see the whole picture: I'd been running a full-service emotional, financial, and household resort, and my children were strolling around with all-inclusive wristbands while I was clocking 24-hour shifts.

So I tried something new.

I didn't slam the fridge.
I didn't go on a monologue about being unappreciated.
I didn't start clanging pots to make a point.

I simply said, calmly:

"Dinner will be ready when everyone has pitched in."

Period. No extra explanation. No nervous laugh. No speech.

At first, there was confusion.
Then a little attitude.

Then the magic sentence every over-functioning parent needs to hear:

"...What do you want me to do?"

Right there, in that small shift from *"What are you serving me?"* to *"What can I do?"*—I felt my crown slide back onto my head.

Not a crown of control.
A crown of calm leadership.

That day, I stopped running the resort and started running a home.

The Silent Signs You're Over-Functioning

Let's put some language to what you might be feeling. You may be over-functioning in your home if:

You're exhausted even when nothing "big" happened today.
The day was normal, but you feel like you ran a marathon no one saw.

You're quietly resentful because your child assumes you'll pick up the slack.
They "forget" their responsibilities because they know you'll remember.

Your boundaries are clear—but your follow-through is foggy.
You give great speeches about responsibility... and then still do the work yourself.

Your child uses you as their Plan A, B, C, and D.
Missed the bus, forgot the assignment, didn't do the chore?
You're their emergency contact for everything.

You feel guilty when you rest.
Sitting down feels like you're doing something wrong.

You feel anxious saying no.
You rehearse the "no" in your head ten times before it comes out of your mouth once.

You love them deeply but feel invisible in your own home.
Everyone knows what you do for them. Few people ask how you are doing.

Over-functioning is not love — it's imbalance.
And imbalance creates entitlement.

The Crown Rule

Here is the rule that changed my motherhood:

"If I'm doing everything, I'm teaching them nothing."

Say it again, Saint.

Children don't grow when you over-function.

They grow when you give them three things:

Space – room to try, fail, and try again

Structure – clear expectations and consequences

Expectation – the belief that they *can* do it, and they *will* do it

When you grab every task, you rob them of practice.
When you snatch every consequence, you rob them of wisdom.
When you rush in to fix every discomfort, you rob them of resilience.

Your job is not to remove every bump.
Your job is to teach them how to walk.

You are not raising a gray-haired toddler. You're raising a future adult.

How to Reclaim Your Crown

You don't have to make a dramatic announcement. You don't need a family summit with printed agendas. Reclaiming your crown is a series of small, firm adjustments in how you show up.

Let's walk through five.

1. Sit Down

Yes, literally.

If you never stop moving, your family never has to start.

The next time you finish your basic responsibilities for the day, sit down. Not with a side eye, not with loud sighs, not with muttering under your breath—just sit.

Let them see you reading a book.
Let them see you watching a show.
Let them see you drinking water like a human being, not a background worker.

When they say, "Mom, where's my...?" try:

"I'm sitting down right now. Check the last place you had it."

When they say, "Can you...?" try:

"Not right now. I'm resting. You can start it, and if you still need help later, I'll see."

Your family needs exposure therapy—to your rest.

They need to learn that your body is not public property and your time is not bottomless.

Sitting down isn't laziness.
It's leadership.

2. Reassign the Load

If you've always carried it, you may not realize how heavy it really is.

Take a quiet moment and make a list:

Laundry

Dishes

Trash

Bathrooms

Floors

Pet care

Rides and errands

Calendar reminders

School forms and deadlines

Lunches and snacks

Now ask:

Which of these are age-appropriate for my kids to share or own completely?

Then start the transfer.

Laundry is no longer "Mom's job." Teens can sort, wash, and fold their own. Younger kids can at least sort and put away.

The kitchen belongs to a rotation: one on dishes, one on counters, one on sweeping.

Trash rotates by week or by room.

Errands get divided: "If you want that extra trip, you're responsible for planning how and when."

When you reassign the load, don't over-explain. Keep it simple:

"You're older now. Part of living here is contributing here. This is your new job."

You're not punishing them.
You're preparing them.

3. Require Follow-Through

This is where most over-functioning parents slide back into old habits.

We say, "Chores first, then phone,"
and then we hand over the phone "just this once" because we're tired of arguing.

We say, "No car until grades improve,"
and then we make an exception because we feel bad.

We say, "I'm not loaning any more money,"
and then we Cash App on the low because we don't want to hear the disappointment.

Here's the truth:

If your boundaries have no follow-through, your child is not confused.
They are taking notes.

Tie privileges to contribution:

No chores = no rides, no spending money, no Wi-Fi code.

Late tasks = late privileges.

Not as revenge, but as reality.

You can say:

"In this house, you don't get premium privileges with bare-minimum effort.
When you show up, the extras show up.
When you don't, they don't.
That's not me being mean—that's me being honest."

You're not raising a gray-haired toddler. You're raising a future adult.

4. Detach From the Reaction

Once you start reclaiming your crown, prepare for the pushback.

There will be eye rolls.
Heavy sighs.
Mini speeches.
Sudden amnesia about every conversation you've had.

That's okay.

Your job is not to regulate their feelings for them.
Your job is to regulate your response.

When the complaints start, remind yourself:

"Their reaction is about their comfort level,
not my worth and not my wisdom."

You can respond with calm phrases like:

"I hear you don't like it. The plan still stands."

"You're allowed to feel frustrated. You're not allowed to be disrespectful."

"I love you. The answer is still no."

Your crown doesn't wobble just because they whine.

Detachment doesn't mean you stop caring. It means you stop letting their emotions drive your decisions.

5. Model Calm Leadership

Your children are learning more from how you carry your crown than from any speech you give.

If you set a boundary and then yell through it, they learn that boundaries equal drama.
If you set a boundary and then cave under tears, they learn that persistence beats policy.

But if you set a boundary and stand in it quietly, they learn something powerful:

"My parent loves me enough to tell me the truth...
and stay steady while I struggle with it."

Calm leadership looks like:

Lowering your voice instead of raising it.

Pausing before you answer.

Saying, "I'll get back to you," and actually taking time to think.

Admitting when you're overwhelmed and taking a break.

You don't have to perform perfection.
You just have to be honest and consistent.

Remember:

A parent who leads calmly, leads effectively.

AUDIT

Take a breath and grab a pen. Let's bring this home.

Where am I over-functioning in my home?

What job am I doing that my child should be doing—or at least helping with regularly?

What is ONE responsibility I will hand back today?

Not ten. Not twenty. One.

Maybe it's their laundry.
Maybe it's the trash.
Maybe it's their lunch.
Maybe it's chasing their school deadlines.

Choose one area and step back—on purpose, on principle, and on repeat.

PRAYER

Lord, help me lead from strength, not exhaustion.
Remind me that raising capable children requires releasing unnecessary burdens.
Show me where I'm doing too much and where I need to step back in faith.
Give me courage to sit in my authority, even when they don't like my boundaries.
Teach my children to see my rest as wisdom, not weakness.
Amen.

TRUTH BOMB

When you stop over-functioning, your child starts maturing.

FINAL SAINT LINE

Sit back down — your crown fits better when you're not bending.

CHAPTER ELEVEN
The reset room: rebuilding the household atmosphere

I created the Reset Room by accident.

One afternoon, the energy in my home was just... off.

Nobody was screaming. No doors were slamming. There was no big "incident" we could point to. But the mood was thick—irritated attitudes, sharp tones, everyone walking around carrying invisible clouds. Even I felt drained, snapping over small things and then feeling guilty five minutes later.

It wasn't a war.
It was a slow leak of peace.

Dishes clinked louder than they needed to.
Replies came short and flat.
People moved past each other like coworkers instead of family.

I walked down the hallway and actually *felt* the tension sitting in the air. You know that feeling when the whole house is on edge, but nobody wants to say it out loud? The little things—unwashed dishes, short replies, heavy footsteps—were stacking up in the corners like clutter.

I stepped into my bedroom, closed the door, sat on the edge of the bed and whispered:

"God, this atmosphere is off."

Immediately, I knew this wasn't about one child, one chore, or one bad day. It was the *vibe*. The whole house felt like it needed a deep breath and a reset.

Not another lecture.
Not another round of blame.
Not another night of everybody hiding in their own room.

A reset.

So instead of calling a "family meeting" (which, let's be honest, sounds like court), I called something different in my spirit:

A family reset.

Not a meeting.
Not a trial.
A reset.

Why Atmosphere Matters More Than You Think

Before I tell you what we did, let's talk about why this even matters.

Your child may not remember every rule you set, but they will never forget the *atmosphere* of their home.

Was it tense or calm?

Was it full of sarcasm or dignity?

Was it a place where people tiptoed… or exhaled?

We tend to get busy managing schedules, grades, chores, and curfews, but the *air* of the house—the tone, the energy, the way we talk and move around each other—teaches just as loudly.

A tense home teaches kids to walk on eggshells.
A chaotic home teaches kids to stay detached.
A peaceful home teaches kids that conflict can
exist *with* respect.

The Reset Room wasn't about pretending everything was okay. It was about saying:

"We can feel this tension, and we are not going to live like this."

How the Reset Room Was Born

I walked back out, still feeling that heaviness, and instead of retreating into my own corner, I did something different.

I called everybody in.

"Come to the table," I said. "Just for a minute."

There was eye contact. Confusion. A little suspicion.

No one was in big trouble, and they knew it—that was part of what made this moment different. I wasn't slamming cabinets or launching into a speech. I was calm.

Everyone sat down.

I took a breath and said one sentence:

"Our energy is off, and we're going to fix it together."

Not:

"Y'all are getting on my nerves."
"Somebody better fix this attitude."
"I'm sick of this house."

Just awareness, spoken out loud.

Our energy is off.
We're going to fix it *together*.

You could feel everyone's shoulders drop one inch. It wasn't a prosecution. It was an invitation.

Right there at that table, without fancy charts or a four-week curriculum, the Reset Room was born.

Not because of the furniture.
Because of the intention.

What the Reset Room Actually Is (and Is Not)

Let's clear this up:

The Reset Room is not:

A punishment room

A "time-out" corner for one perpetually "bad" child

A courtroom where you replay every fight

A place where only the kids get corrected while the adults go free

The Reset Room is:

A neutral space in your home

A place where the whole family can pause and reset the atmosphere

A judgment-free zone to acknowledge, "Something's off"

A tool to interrupt tension *before* it becomes a blowup

In my house, the Reset Room eventually became an actual space—a particular corner of the living room with a lamp, soft lighting, and a couple of chairs. But at the beginning, it was just the dining table and a decision:

We are not going to keep walking past this tension like it's normal.

You don't need a new couch or a Pinterest board to create a Reset Room. You need:

A place

A tone

A plan

The plan is simple.

The Four-Step Reset

That day, we reset with four steps. Simple on purpose, so anyone could remember them—even the teens. Especially the teens.

I didn't roll it out like a workshop. I just led one step at a time.

RESET STEP 1: Identify the Pattern

I started with one question:

"What's been happening around here this week?"

Then I waited.

Not staring anybody down. Not answering for them. Not turning it into a sermon.

I let them think.

Little by little, things came out:

"People keep snapping at each other."

"Nobody's really talking, we're just in our rooms."

"The house is a mess and it makes me not want to be in here."

"I feel like you're mad all the time."

"We don't finish conversations; we just walk away."

We weren't arguing our cases; we were naming patterns.

Common patterns sound like:

Too much attitude

Too little communication

Disrespect

Mess

Avoidance

Tone

Clutter

Chaos

It wasn't about who started it. It was about what was *happening*.

MINI TRUTH BOMB:

You can't reset what you're not willing to name.

Awareness creates unity: "We all feel this. We are all living in it. So we all get to shift it."

RESET STEP 2: Everyone Owns One Thing

Next, I said:

"Okay. Everybody owns one thing. Not ten. One."

That was the rule—*one* thing each of us would take ownership of.

I went first, because leadership goes first.

"I need to stop letting my frustration leak into my tone," I said. "I'm tired, but I have to own my delivery."

Then they followed:

"I need to stop snapping."

"I need to clean my room instead of pretending I don't see it."

"I need to stop walking away when someone calls my name."

"I need to talk earlier instead of letting things build."

Not:

"I need to stop being a terrible person."
"I need to never make a mistake again."

Just one behavior. One pattern. One choice.

MINI TRUTH BOMB:
When everyone owns something, no one has to be the villain.

Ownership creates humility. It breaks the "it's all your fault" cycle and turns it into, "We all have work to do."

RESET STEP 3: Set One Household Standard

Then we set one standard.

Not ten new rules. Not a full policy manual. Just one clear line we could all remember.

Standards sound like:

"In this house, we talk to each other respectfully the first time."

"No dirty dishes overnight in the sink."

"No yelling after 9 PM."

"Phones off at dinner."

That day, we chose a simple one:

"In this house, we don't talk to each other like strangers."

That covered tone. Disrespect. Distance. Coldness.

Yours might be:

"In this house, we clean up what we mess up."

or

"In this house, we look people in the eye when they're talking to us."

One standard resets the entire home.

You're not trying to rebuild the whole house in a day. You're picking one brick and placing it straight.

RESET STEP 4: Pray Together or Pause Together

Last step.

If your family prays, this is where you invite God into the atmosphere on purpose.

If not, this is where you do one minute of silence—phones down, eyes closed, everyone breathing.

That day, we prayed. It wasn't a long, theatrical prayer. Just something like:

"God, help us fix what we just named. Help us talk better. Help us see each other. Help this house feel like home again."

The power wasn't in perfect words. It was in the act of coming together around a shared desire:

"We want peace in this house."

If you choose silence instead, you might say:

"We're just going to sit for one minute and breathe. No talking. Just calm."

Resetting together creates unity.

You're telling your kids:

"We don't just correct each other separately. We heal together."

How to Set Up Your Own Reset Room

Don't overthink this. You don't need HGTV to bless it.

Here's all you really need:

A physical spot

A corner of the living room

The dining table

A section of the couch

Even your porch, if that's where people can sit without distractions

A visual cue

A small candle you only light for resets

A specific blanket or pillow

A simple sign that says "Reset"

The point isn't decor. It's *signal*. When this light is on, we're in reset mode—not attack mode.

Three ground rules

No blame

No interruptions

No fixing everything at once

You can introduce it like this:

"From now on, when I say, 'Reset Room,' it just means we're going to pause, sit together, and check the atmosphere. Not to punish anybody, but to protect our peace."

Make it clear: anyone can call a reset—kids included.

If your teen says, "I think we need a reset," that's not disrespect. That's emotional maturity.

When the Reset Room Starts to Work

The first time will feel a little awkward. That's okay. New things usually do.

You might get:

Nervous laughter

Shrugs

"This is weird."

You can respond:

"It's okay if it feels weird. What we've been doing hasn't been working. Let's try something better."

Over time, here's what begins to shift:

People start catching their own tone faster.

Arguments shorten because you have a shared language: "We need a reset."

Kids feel safer naming tension instead of stuffing it.

You stop letting bad moods linger for days.

The house won't turn into a spa overnight. But you'll start noticing small changes:

Laughter creeps back in.
Little kind gestures show up again.
People say, "good morning" and sound like they mean it.

The Reset Room becomes a gentle promise:

"No matter how off today feels, we can always start again."

AUDIT

Does my home feel tense, chaotic, or heavy more often than I'd like to admit?

What pattern keeps repeating in our atmosphere—attitude, silence, sarcasm, mess, avoidance?

What one standard do we need to reset as a family this week?

PRAYER

God, restore the atmosphere of my home.
Replace tension with peace and frustration with unity.
Show us the patterns we need to name and the standards we need to reset.
Help us pause before we explode, and choose connection over conflict.
Teach us to reset with love, humility, and honesty—together.

Amen.

TRUTH BOMB

A home out of order needs a reset, not a war.

FINAL SAINT LINE

Reset the room, and the hearts inside it will follow.

CHAPTER TWELVE
Policy beats pleading: systems that run your home

There comes a point in parenting when you realize you're not running a home anymore...
you're running a customer service center.

You're repeating the same lines:
"How many times do I have to say this?"
"I'm not going to tell you again."
"Why is this house ALWAYS like this?"

And yet... you *do* tell them again.
And the house *is* like this.
And your voice is tired.

That's not because you're a bad parent.
It's because you're working with pleading, not policy.

Pleading says:

"Can you PLEASE clean your room?"

Policy says:

"Rooms are clean by Friday at 6. If not, privileges pause until it's done."

Pleading is emotional.
Policy is clear.

Pleading makes you the nag.
Policy makes you the leader.

And Saint, you were not called to be the household's emotional Roomba—rolling around picking up everything and everybody. You were called to lead.

Pleading vs. Policy: What's Really Happening

Let's keep it all the way real.

Pleading sounds like:

"Can you PLEASE clean your room?"

"I'm tired of repeating myself."

"Why won't you just LISTEN?"

"If I have to say this one more time…"

It's desperate.
It's emotional.
And it trains your child to wait for volume instead of respecting values.

In a pleading home:

Kids move when your *voice* spikes, not when the *expectation* exists.

Chores get done when you're about to snap, not when they're actually due.

Your nervous system is running the whole show.

Now let's flip it.

Policy sounds like:

"Rooms must be clean by Friday at 6."

"If the kitchen isn't clean by 8 PM, privileges pause until tomorrow."

"Phones dock at 10."

"We don't yell in this house. If it happens, the conversation ends until we're calm."

Policy is calm, clear, and consistent.

You don't beg.
You don't bargain.
You don't broadcast your stress.

You state the standard.
You state the consequence.
You follow through.

And then you go sit down with your crown on.

TRUTH BOMB

If you keep rescuing with your emotions, they'll keep ignoring your words.

Why Your Home Feels Chaotic (And It's Not Because of the Kids)

When homes feel out of control, we blame:

The teen's attitude

The little one's mess

The schedule

The phones

But underneath all of that is one simple fact:

You're trying to manage patterns with feelings instead of systems.

You're out here:

Negotiating bedtimes every night

Debating chores like it's a group project

Arguing about phones in real time

Begging for help you already asked for ten times

That's not a home problem.
That's a system problem.

Policies do three powerful things:

They predict – Everyone knows what's coming.

They protect – You don't have to fight every little battle.

They parent – The system does the heavy lifting so you can be the heart, not the hallway monitor.

When expectations are written, repeated, and enforced calmly, you're no longer the villain in every story. You're the leader of a team that knows the playbook.

Think Systems, Not Slogans

A lot of parents have "house sayings":

"We respect each other here."

"We don't do disrespect."

"We're a team in this house."

Those are cute.

But without systems, they're just slogans on a Pinterest board.

A system is:

Specific

Predictable

Connected to action and consequence

Example:

Slogan: "We clean up after ourselves."

System: "Every dish must be rinsed and in the dishwasher by 8 PM. If not, no TV/phone until the kitchen is reset."

See the difference?
One sounds nice.
The other actually runs your home.

MINI TRUTH BOMB

Policies are just house values with teeth.

Policy vs. Punishment

Before we go deeper, hear this:

Policy is not punishment.
It's preparation.

Punishment says:

"I'm mad, so I'll make you pay."

Policy says:

"We agreed. You chose. Here's what that choice unlocks."

In a punishment home:

Consequences swing with your mood.

Kids feel blindsided.

You feel guilty afterward.

In a policy home:

The rule was clear.

The consequence was known.

Your tone stays low and steady, even when they're loud.

You don't have to yell when the policy already speaks.

The Core Shift: From "Please" to "Policy"

Here's the mindset reset:

Instead of:

"How many times do I have to ask you?"

You move to:

"You know the policy. What did you choose?"

Instead of:

"I don't understand why this room looks like this."

You move to:

"It's Friday at 6. The room isn't done. That means no rides / Wi-Fi / game until it is."

Instead of:

"Why won't you just respect me?"

You move to:

"In this house, we talk respectfully the first time. If that doesn't happen, the conversation ends, and privileges pause."

Policies are emotional seatbelts.

They hold you steady when your child's reaction tries to throw you back into old patterns.

System 1: The Three-Strike Reset

You do not have to jump from calm to chaos in 0.3 seconds.

Use the Three-Strike Reset:

Strike 1: Reminder
Calm, short, neutral.

"Remember the policy: dishes done by 8 PM."

Strike 2: Warning
Clearly name the consequence.

"If dishes aren't done in 10 minutes, Wi-Fi pauses until tomorrow."

Strike 3: Consequence
Follow through. No speeches.

"Time's up. Wi-Fi is paused. You can try again tomorrow."

Not emotional.
Not a debate.
Just structure.

If they argue?

"We can talk when you're calm. The consequence stands."

Your job is not to make them like the policy.
Your job is to live it.

System 2: The Phone Dock Rule

Let's talk about the glowing rectangle that is raising half the children on earth: phones.

Phones are not evil.

But unstructured phones create:

Exhausted kids

Fried attention spans

Disrespectful attitudes

Late-night chaos

You don't fix that with shouting.
You fix it with policy.

Phone Dock Rule:

"All phones dock at 10 PM in the kitchen. No exceptions. No arguing."

You can adjust the time for your house, but the core stays:

One location.

One time.

One standard.

If a phone doesn't dock?

It's gone the next day. Period.

No texting friends about how unfair you are from under the covers.

No "just this once."

And yes, —your phone too.

You're modeling the policy, not monitoring from the couch, scrolling until 2 a.m.

MINI TRUTH BOMB

If the phones don't have a bedtime, neither do their attitudes.

System 3: The Chore Rotation Board

If you are the only one doing chores in a home full of capable humans...

that's not love. That's unpaid overtime.

We fix that with a Chore Rotation Board.

Step 1: List the core jobs

Kitchen

Trash & recycling

Floors

Bathroom wipe-down

Laundry help (not all the laundry—*help*)

Step 2: Assign by week

Put a simple chart on the wall:

Week 1: Name Kitchen Trash Floors Laundry Help

1

Rotate every week. Older kids can take heavier zones; younger kids get simpler tasks.

Step 3: Attach privilege

"No chores, no extras."

No rides

No gaming

No special outings

No cash requests

Not punishment—policy.

If someone doesn't do their part?

"Your zone isn't done, so your extra is paused. You can earn it back when your job is complete."

You're training them for real life, where rent, bills, and responsibilities don't disappear because someone "wasn't feeling it."

System 4: The "Ask, Don't Assist" Rule

You know that child who will yell your name from three rooms away:

"Mooooom! I can't find my hoodie!"
"Mooooom! The Wi-Fi isn't working!"
"Mooooom! I need you right now!"

You are not Siri.

We're retiring the default servant role.

Ask, Don't Assist Rule:

You do not assist until they ask respectfully.

If the tone is off?

You calmly say:

"Try that again with respect. I'm happy to help when you speak to me kindly."

If they roll their eyes or refuse?

"Then I'm not the right person to help you right now."

This teaches:

Respectful communication

Emotional regulation

The simple fact that access to you is valuable

Your love is unconditional.
Your access is not.

System 5: The No-Fix Rule

This one is going to pinch a little.

If they forget:

Homework

Lunch

Gym shoes

Project

Charger

You. Do. Not. Fix. It.

You do not:

Leave work.

Burn gas.

Rearrange your whole day.

Negotiate with every teacher like a defense attorney.

You say:

"That's tough. What's your plan for next time?"

Natural consequences are not cruelty.
They are curriculum.

The first time they sit hungry, embarrassed, or unprepared, a new part of their brain wakes up:

"I need a system so this doesn't happen again."

And guess what? That's executive functioning, not "meanness."

TRUTH BOMB
If you fix every problem, you also fix their chance to grow.

How to Roll Out Policy Without Starting a War

You don't drop all this in one night like a new law from Congress.

You introduce systems in calm moments, not in conflict.

Step 1: Call a Calm "House Reset," Not a Hearing

No one wants to feel on trial.

You might say:

"I've noticed our home feels tense and chaotic. I've been nagging and repeating myself, and I don't like the parent I am when I'm constantly pleading. I'm making some changes so we can all breathe and live better together."

Short. Honest. Calm.

Then introduce one system at a time:

Week 1: Phone Dock Rule

Week 2: Chore Rotation

Week 3: Three-Strike Reset

Week 4: No-Fix Rule

Step 2: Explain, Don't Apologize

You're not asking for permission to lead.

You're saying:

"This is the new policy. I know it will feel different at first, but I believe this will help all of us."

Step 3: Expect Pushback… and Stay Seated

There will be:

Eye rolls

Sighs

"This is dumb."

"No one else's mom does this."

Your line:

"You're allowed to have feelings. The policy still stands."

You are not negotiating the existence of the policy.
You're teaching them how to move through
their feelings about it.

Policy with Teens and Gray-Haired Toddlers

This isn't just for little ones.

Your adult kids? They need policy even more.

Instead of:

"Why don't you ever help around here?"

You move to:

"If you live here, you contribute. That means:
• Rent / groceries / utilities by the 1st, or
• 10 hours a week of house contribution (childcare, cooking, errands, etc.).
No contribution, no keys. That's the policy."

Instead of:

"You can't keep coming in at 3 a.m. and waking up the whole house."

You move to:

"House policy: Everyone in by midnight on weeknights. If not, the door is locked, and you need to arrange your own place to stay. I love you. I'm done sacrificing sleep and safety."

Policy is how you stop being emotionally blackmailed by grown people you fed, clothed, and prayed over.

You're not being cruel.
You're teaching them how the world actually works.

Making Policy Visible

Policies work best when they are:

Simple

Written

Visible

This is not a courtroom. You don't need a 12-page legal code on the fridge. But you do need something like:

Family Policy Board

Phone Dock: All devices in the kitchen by 10 PM.

Kitchen Reset: Dishes done and counters wiped by 8 PM.

Chores: Check the weekly rotation.

Respect Rule: No yelling, cursing, or name-calling. If it happens, the conversation ends and privileges pause.

No-Fix Rule: We don't rescue forgotten items. Natural consequences teach responsibility.

You can make it cute, color-coded, or just black and white.

The power is not in the fonts.
It's in the follow-through.

When You Break Your Own Policy

Let's be honest. You're human.

You will:

Cave sometimes.

Rescue once in a while.

Forget to dock your own phone.

Let a chore slide because you're tired.

When that happens, don't spiral into shame. Just reset.

You can say:

"I broke my own policy yesterday. That's on me. I'm getting back on track today."

You're modeling accountability, not perfection.

Kids learn more from watching you correct yourself than watching you pretend you never slip.

What Policies Actually Give You

This isn't about creating a boot camp.
It's about creating peace.

Policies give you:

Fewer repeating arguments

Clear boundaries around your time and energy

A calmer nervous system

Kids who understand that actions have predictable outcomes

A home that feels less like chaos and more like order with love

Instead of screaming into the void, you'll find yourself saying:

"You know the policy."
"You made a choice."
"You can try again tomorrow."

And then you go sit down, sip your tea, and let the system work.

BIG TRUTH BOMB
Families don't rise on rules — they rise on systems.

Rules tell them what not to do.
Systems show them how to live.

AUDIT

Where Does Policy Need to Replace Pleading?

Take a breath and be honest with yourself:

Where am I over-talking instead of setting a policy?

What rule causes the most arguing, tears, or tension in our home?

Where am I secretly hoping they'll change without me changing the system?

What is ONE system I can implement this week—Phone Dock, Chore Rotation, Three-Strike Reset, No-Fix Rule?

Write it down.
Pick one.
Start there.

REFLECT & RESET

Legacy Question:
What kind of home do I want my child to remember—one full of chaos and yelling, or one where expectations were clear and love had structure?

Trust Question:
How can I use policies and systems to balance love and discipline in a way my child can trust, even when they don't like the consequences?

Today's Tweak:
What is one pleading script I will retire today—and what policy statement will I replace it with?

PRAYER

Lord,
Help me lead my home with clarity and structure,
not exhaustion and pleading.
Replace chaos with order, and shouting with steady, calm leadership.

Show me the systems our family needs,
and give me the courage to follow through.
Teach my children that consequences are not cruelty, but preparation.
Let our home be a place where peace is protected by wise policies,
and where love and responsibility walk hand in hand.
Amen.

TRUTH BOMB

Families don't rise on rules — they rise on systems.

FINAL SAINT LINE

Set the policy and watch the peace return.

CHAPTER THIRTEEN
Emotional sobriety: parenting without panic or pleasing

There's a moment in parenting when you realize:
You're not just tired in your body...
you're tired in your feelings.

You're drained from:

Walking on eggshells around your child's moods

Apologizing just to keep the peace

Saying yes when everything in you is screaming no

Crying in the shower because you feel guilty either way

That's emotional intoxication.

You're not drunk on alcohol—you're drunk on:

Guilt

Fear

Over-responsibility

The need to be liked by your own child

And when you're emotionally intoxicated, your parenting looks like this:

You overreact... or you over-explain

You chase their approval

You crumble when they're mad at you

You make decisions from panic or pleasing, not from peace

Emotional sobriety is the opposite.

Emotional sobriety means you parent from clarity, not from emotional chaos.
You feel your feelings.
You see their feelings.
But you let values, not emotions, drive the car.

You can hug them and still hold the boundary.
You can care deeply and still say, "No, that's not happening."
You can love your child… without letting their reactions run your house.

What Emotional Sobriety Really Is (And What It's Not)

Let's clear this up first.

Emotional sobriety does *not* mean:

You never cry

You never get triggered

You float around like some Zen robot who never raises an eyebrow

You're human. You will feel things.

Emotional sobriety *does* mean:

You notice your feelings before you act

You pause instead of popping off

You make decisions from your values, not your fear

You can handle your child's disappointment without collapsing

Sobriety isn't the absence of emotion.
It's the leadership of emotion.

Emotions are supposed to be indicators, not navigators.
They can tell you what's happening—
but they don't get to tell you what to do.

When you're emotionally sober as a parent, you:

Respond instead of reacting

Listen without losing yourself

Hold the line without hating yourself afterward

You become the calm spine your home has been begging for.

Emotional Intoxication: When Feelings Drive the Car

Let's name it, because some of us grew up in this.

Emotional intoxication looks like:

Yelling, slamming, or crying every time there's conflict

Over-giving money, time, rides, and second chances because you feel guilty

Avoiding boundaries because you're scared, they'll pull away

Saying, "Forget it, I'll do it," just to stop the tension

Chasing your child's mood like it's a weather report you have to fix

You might recognize these patterns:

You overreact to little things because your tank is empty

You apologize when they were the one out of line

You let your child's sulking talk you out of your own decisions

You lose sleep replaying what you said, wondering if you were "too harsh"

That's not just parenting.
That's emotional over-functioning.

You're doing all the emotional labor—managing:

Your feelings

Their feelings

Everyone else's comfort

...while your own needs are sitting in the corner like, "Um. Hello?"

TRUTH BOMB
If you're always the emotional firefighter, you start attracting fires.

When Panic and Pleasing Run the House

Most of us slide into emotional intoxication from two places:

Panic – "What if I mess them up?"

Pleasing – "I don't want them to be mad at me."

So we parent from:

Fear of losing the relationship

Fear they'll "never come back"

Fear they'll say, "You were a bad mom" one day

Or we parent from:

A deep need to be liked

Old childhood wounds where nobody protected us

Guilt because we weren't perfect when they were younger

Listen to me:

You can love your child and still be their parent.
You can be nurturing and still say, "Absolutely not."

Emotional sobriety is what lets you do both.

How Emotional Sobriety Connects to Policy and Systems

In the last chapter, we built systems:

Phone Dock

Chore Rotation

No-Fix Rule

Three-Strike Reset

Ask, Don't Assist

Those policies don't work if your emotions are drunk.

Because what good is:

"All phones dock at 10"
...if at 10:07 you cave because they're "talking to a friend who needs them"?

What good is:

"No rides if chores aren't done"
…if you're still driving them around because you feel bad?

Emotional sobriety is the muscle that lets you hold the system.

Policy says:

"This is the standard."

Sobriety says:

"I can handle your feelings about it."

Policy without sobriety becomes flexible in all the wrong places.
Sobriety without policy becomes quiet strength with no plan.

You need both:

Systems to guide the home

A sober parent to hold the line

Emotional Sobriety in Real Time: The Three-Second Pause

Let's get practical.

Here's what emotional sobriety looks like in the *moment*:

Step 1: Notice the Spike

You feel it:

Heart racing

Stomach tight

Jaw clenching

Heat in your face

That "I'm about to go OFF" feeling

Instead of pushing through, you name it silently:

"I'm triggered."

"My body is activated."

"My emotions are loud right now."

Step 2: Take the Three-Second Pause

Before you speak:

Inhale slowly for 3 seconds

Exhale slowly for 3–4 seconds

Drop your shoulders

Unclench your jaw

While you're breathing, you ask yourself:

"What do I want to model right now?"

"What does sober parenting look like in this moment?"

You don't need a 20-minute meditation.
You just need three honest seconds of awareness.

Step 3: Lead with a Calm Sentence

Instead of matching their chaos, you say:

"I hear you. I'm not changing the boundary."

"We can talk when your voice is calm."

"I love you. The answer is still no."

"You're allowed to be upset. The policy stands."

Short. Steady. Sober.

MINI TRUTH BOMB
Sometimes emotional sobriety is just the courage to shut your mouth for three seconds before you speak.

When You're Emotionally Sober, You Don't…

When you're emotionally sober:

You don't panic.

You don't overreact.

You don't overgive.

You don't crumble under guilt.

You don't match your child's energy.

You are the thermostat, not the thermometer.

They can slam.
They can stomp.
They can sigh and roll their eyes all the way to heaven.

You can still calmly say:

"I hear your frustration. The boundary isn't moving."

That's sobriety.

Sign 1: You Apologize Too Quickly

You know this one.

Your child raises their voice…
and you fold like a lawn chair.

They say:

"You're doing too much."

"I hate this house."

"You always take it too far."

"You're ruining my life."

Suddenly you're doubting yourself:

"Maybe I *am* doing too much."

"Maybe I should ease up."

"Maybe I overreacted."

So without them changing a single behavior, you rush in with:

"I'm sorry, I just want what's best."

"Forget it, it's fine—just go."

"Okay, okay, just this once."

That's not healthy humility.
That's emotional intoxication.

Sobriety sounds like:

"I hear that you're upset. I'm not apologizing for the boundary."

"I love you. I'm okay if you're mad. The rule still stands."

"We can talk about *how* I said it. But the *what* is not changing."

Apology is for when you were truly wrong, not when they're just loud.

You can absolutely say:

"I was too harsh in my tone. I do apologize for that. But the consequence remains."

That's sober. That's grown. That's parenting.

Sign 2: You Fear Their Reactions

If you've ever thought:

"I don't want to bring this up; they'll explode."

"If I set this rule, they might stop talking to me."

"If I say no, they'll run to the other parent or grandparents."

...that's fear driving.

When you fear their reactions, you start:

Lowering your standards

Avoiding necessary conversations

Saying yes because you don't want "drama"

But here's the hard truth:

If their reaction controls your decisions, your peace is on a leash.

Emotional sobriety says:

"I can handle your disappointment."

"Your reaction is yours. My decision is mine."

"I'm not scared of you being upset. I'm scared of not preparing you for real life."

You're not starting a war.
You're ending a hostage situation—where your nervous system is tied to your child's mood.

MINI TRUTH BOMB
If you tiptoe around their reactions, you're teaching them their feelings are weapons.
Sobriety puts the weapons down.

Sign 3: You Make Decisions Based on Their Mood

You know emotional intoxication is in the building when:

They're in a good mood → you say yes to things you don't mean

They're in a bad mood → you avoid boundaries you know you need

You're constantly "reading the room" instead of leading the room

You think:

"She's finally being nice—let me not ruin it with rules."

"He's already mad—this is not the time to bring that up."

So your whole parenting strategy becomes:

"Don't rock the boat."

But...

Their mood fluctuates.

Your values should not.

Sobriety sounds like:

"I'm glad we're having a good day. That doesn't change the policy."

"Even though this may upset you, I still need to address it."

"Your mood matters to me, but it doesn't manage me."

Sobriety breaks the leash.

You stop making decisions based on

"Are they happy with me right now?"

and start asking

"Is this aligned with who I'm called to be as a parent?"

Sign 4: You Over-Explain

Emotional intoxication loves a long sermon.

Your teen pushes back, and suddenly you're in a:

40-minute TED Talk

7-paragraph text message

3-part follow-up conversation

You're trying to:

Convince

Convict

Convert

…instead of simply communicating.

You want them to understand so badly that you forget:

They don't need to agree for the boundary to be valid.

A sober parent uses 10-word sentences, not TED Talks.

"Because that's the rule. We'll revisit later."

"No screens after 10. That's house policy."

"Ride canceled. You didn't follow through."

"You can be mad. The answer's still no."

Short. Clear. Calm.

You are not on trial.
You are not the defendant.
You are the parent.

MINI TRUTH BOMB
Over-explaining is often a sign you don't feel allowed to lead. Sobriety says: "I'm allowed."

Sign 5: You Take Everything Personally

This one is heavy.

They roll their eyes.
You feel disrespected in your soul.

They sigh.
You hear, "You're a failure."

They slam the door.
You feel like the worst parent alive.

Hear me:

Their eye rolls aren't a referendum on your worth.

Their sighs aren't performance reviews.

Their bad day is not your entire identity.

Sobriety separates:

Their mood from your identity

Their behavior from your leadership

Instead of:

"Why do you treat me like this? After everything I've done?"

Sobriety responds with:

"I don't like how you spoke to me. Try that again."

"I see you're upset. You still can't slam doors here."

"I love you too much to let this attitude run the house."

You correct the behavior, not collapse as a person.

You stop assigning your worth to their reactions and start rooting it in:

Your calling

Your values

Your growth

You are more than their last mood.

Practical Tools for Emotional Sobriety

Let's put some handles on this.
Here's how you build emotional sobriety day by day.

Tool 1: The Internal Check-In

Before you respond, ask yourself:

"What am I feeling right now—anger, fear, guilt, shame?"

"Is this about them... or is this touching an old wound in me?"

"If I weren't scared or guilty, what would I do?"

You don't need a therapist's couch to start this.
Just honest questions in a hard moment.

Tool 2: Script the Sobriety Sentence

Create one go-to sentence for heated moments:

"I need a minute. We'll talk when I'm calmer."

"I hear you. I'm not changing the boundary."

"We can finish this conversation later. The consequence stands."

You're not avoiding the issue; you're refusing to respond while intoxicated.

Tool 3: Use the Reset Room—For You

Remember the Reset Room from earlier?
It's not just for the kids.

Sometimes the most sober move is to say:

"I'm stepping into the reset space for five minutes. I'll be back."

You breathe.
You pray.
You cry if you need to.

Then you come back with a calm spine.

Tool 4: Pre-Decide the Policy

Emotional intoxication thrives on spur-of-the-moment decisions.

Sobriety thrives on pre-decisions:

"If they miss curfew, the car is parked for a week."

"If chores aren't done, there are no rides that day."

"If voices rise, the conversation pauses for 20 minutes."

When the situation hits, you're not scrambling.
You're simply executing what you already decided in a calm moment.

When Old Wounds Try to Run Your Parenting

A lot of emotional intoxication comes from your own story:

Maybe nobody ever listened to you as a child,
so now you over-listen and under-lead.

Maybe discipline in your home was harsh,
so now you're scared to correct at all.

Maybe you grew up walking on eggshells,
so now you're terrified of your own child's anger.

Sobriety doesn't shame you for that.
It just says:

"My past can explain my reactions, but it can't be allowed to run my parenting."

You can tell yourself:

"I'm not parenting mini-me—I'm parenting this child in front of me."

"I won't overcorrect my childhood by under-parenting my own kids."

"I can tolerate their discomfort without abandoning my role."

MINI TRUTH BOMB
Parent the child, not your past.
Emotional sobriety is how you do that.

REFLECT & RESET

Let's bring this home.

Legacy Question
What kind of emotional climate do I want my child to remember?

A parent who panicked, pleaded, and walked on eggshells?

Or a parent who felt deeply and led calmly, even on hard days?

Trust Question
How can I balance empathy and boundaries in a way my child can trust?

Do they know I won't crumble when they're upset?

Do they know my love isn't on trial every time they're disappointed?

Today's Tweak
What's one place I can practice emotional sobriety today?

Holding a small boundary without over-explaining

Saying, "I need a minute" instead of snapping

Not rescuing from a natural consequence

Refusing to apologize for a clear, necessary boundary

Pick one.
Circle it.
Walk it out today—imperfectly, but honestly.

AUDIT

Where am I emotionally intoxicated in my parenting?

What reaction from my child scares me most?

What would sobriety look like for me today—in one decision, one sentence, one boundary?

PRAYER

Lord,
Steady my emotions when the storms hit.
Give me clarity when I want to react,
and courage when I want to please.
Help me parent from wisdom, not fear;
from values, not panic.
Teach me to feel my feelings
without letting them drive my decisions.
Make me a calm spine in my home—
a parent who can love deeply, lead clearly,

and stand firm with grace.
Amen.

TRUTH BOMB

Emotional sobriety is the calm spine your home is waiting for.

FINAL SAINT LINE

Lead from clarity—not from the storm.

CHAPTER FOURTEEN
The respect restoration plan: thirty days back to peace

Respect doesn't disappear overnight—
and it doesn't return overnight.

Most homes don't lose respect in one big explosion.
It leaks out slowly.

One slammed door that slides.

One eye roll you ignore because you're tired.

One curse word under the breath.

One, "Whatever," that you let pass so you don't start a fight.

Week after week, month after month, the tone shifts.
Suddenly you look up and realize:

Your home is loud.
Your body is tense.
Your nerves are fried.

And the worst part?
Disrespect doesn't even feel shocking anymore.
It feels normal.

This chapter is your reset button.

Not a magic wand.
Not a "read this once and everything changes."

It's a 30-day Respect Restoration Plan designed to:

Calm the emotional temperature

Rebuild your leadership

Give your kids clear structures to push against and grow inside

You're not just demanding respect back—
you're teaching it, modeling it, and systematizing it.

This plan works because it's:

Simple

Repetitive

Consistent

Predictable

Kids thrive under predictable leadership.
So do exhausted parents.

Let's walk it out, one week at a time.

HOW TO USE THIS PLAN

You don't need perfection. You need presence.

You don't need a calm house already. You need commitment.

You don't need every child on board on Day 1. You need you anchored.

Think of this as a 30-day "rehab" for your home's emotional climate.
You're detoxing from:

Yelling as a default

Disrespect as a habit

Pleading instead of policy

Chaos instead of structure

You will not get it "right" every day. That's okay.
The win is that you keep coming back.

Big picture, here's the plan:

Week 1 – Tone Reset: Calm the noise.

Week 2 – Responsibility Reset: Reassign the load.

Week 3 – Respect Language Reset: Change how you all talk.

Week 4 – Household Systems Reset: Lock in structure that lasts.

Every week has:

A clear goal

Daily micro-actions

One small win to celebrate

Let's start at the foundation—tone.

WEEK 1 — TONE RESET

Goal: Stop emotional escalation. Calm the room before you fix the room.

This week is not about getting every chore done.
This week is about one thing:

No more riding emotional roller coasters together.

You are teaching:

"We can disagree without destroying the peace."

"We pause before we pop off."

"We lead with tone, not tantrums."

Daily Focus (repeat every day this week)

Use the Safe Word

Agree as a family on one word: *Yellow, Pause, Dragon*—you choose.

When anyone says it (you or them), the conversation pauses, not the consequence.

You step away 10–20 minutes, then return at a set time.

Pause, Not Panic

You feel your voice rising?

Three-second pause.

Inhale. Exhale. Drop your shoulders.

Then answer in one calm sentence, not a 3-minute speech.

Model a Calm Tone

You go first.

Speak slower and softer than the energy coming at you.

If voices rise, you calmly say:

"We can talk when voices are calm."

10-Minute Evening Reset Conversation

Before bed, ask:

"What went well with respect today?"

"What do we want to try different tomorrow?"

No lectures. Two or three sentences each. That's it.

Example Task

On Day 3, your teen rolls their eyes and slams a cabinet. Old you wants to snap, "Who do you think you're talking to?"

New you:

Says the safe word.

Pauses 30 seconds.

Comes back with:

"I hear you're frustrated. We don't slam things here. Try that again with respect."

The disrespect doesn't escalate into a screaming match because you refused to feed the fire.
The boundary stands.
The night stays calmer.

Small win of Week 1:

"Today our home stayed calmer—even if only 10% calmer—because *I* stayed calmer."

WEEK 2 — RESPONSIBILITY RESET

Goal: Reassign the load and expectations. Respect follows contribution.

This is where you stop being the full-time maid, chef, and emotional butler.

In a respectful home, everyone contributes.
You are teaching:

"If you live here, you help here."

Daily Focus (repeat all week)

One Chore Per Child (Minimum)

Age-appropriate and consistent.

Example:

Under 10: toys, trash, setting the table

10–14: dishes, sweeping, bathroom wipes

Teens: laundry, cooking one meal, major zones

One Clear Consequence for Disrespect

You pick it before the drama:

"Disrespectful tone = phone docks for 2 hours."

"Slamming doors = door stays open for the evening."

You don't invent consequences in anger. You execute what you already decided.

One Praise Moment Daily

Find something to notice: effort, tone, follow-through.

"I noticed you took out the trash without me reminding you. That's grown behavior. Thank you."

Respect grows faster in soil where kids feel seen, not just corrected.

Repeat One Household Standard Every Day

Pick one line and say it daily:

"In this house, privilege follows responsibility."

"In this house, we talk to each other with respect."

It becomes the drumbeat of the week.

Example Task

By Day 10, the sink still isn't perfect—but your 16-year-old is loading the dishwasher without reminders three nights out of seven.

On the nights they "forget," you calmly follow through:

"The kitchen isn't done. That means no Wi-Fi tonight. Try again tomorrow."

No lectures.
No yelling.
Just policy doing the heavy lifting.

Respect starts to feel routine, not dramatic.

Small win of Week 2:

"Everyone contributed something today—even if I had to remind them."

WEEK 3 — RESPECT LANGUAGE RESET

Goal: Teach communication that travels outside your front door.

You're not just raising kids who talk nicely to you.
You're raising humans who know how to speak to:

Teachers

Coaches

Bosses

Police

Partners

Their own future children

This week, you zero in on language.

Daily Script Practice

You will feel like a broken record. That's the point.

Use these three scripts every day:

"Try again with respect."

When they snap, mumble, or get slick.

You're not arguing—just offering a redo.

"Speak clearly."

No mumbling from across the room.

"Come to where I am, look at me, and ask again."

"Use a calm voice."

You're teaching tone as part of respect, not extra credit.

Example Task

Your college kid snaps, "Relax, I said I was coming," when you ask about curfew. Old pattern: you match the tone and lecture about disrespect.

New pattern:

You pause and say:

"Try again with respect."

They huff. They roll their eyes.
But they repeat:

"I'll be home by midnight."

Same message.
New delivery.
Nervous systems stay calmer.

You're not just correcting words—you're retraining the muscle of how to talk under pressure.

Small win of Week 3:

"We corrected tone before it turned into full conflict."

WEEK 4 — HOUSEHOLD SYSTEMS RESET

Goal: Replace chaos with structure so respect has somewhere to live.

By now, you've:

Calmed the tone

Reassigned responsibility

Cleaned up the language

Week 4 locks it all in with systems.
Because rules are a paragraph; systems are a lifestyle.

Daily Habits This Week

Phone Docking

Set one clear rule:

"All phones dock in the kitchen by 10 PM. No exceptions."

If a phone doesn't dock?

It's gone the next day. Period.

Chore Rotation

Post a simple chart on the fridge or wall.

Everyone knows their weekly zone. No confusion.

"Check the chart" replaces "Didn't you hear me?"

Early Bedtime Routines (for kids/teens)

Not "lights-out at 7" if you have teens—just consistent wind-down.

Example:

9:30: screens off

10: phones dock

10:30: lights out

Tired kids are disrespectful kids. Rest is respect fuel.

Weekly Family Reset Meeting (15 Minutes, Max)

Pick a day (Sunday night, for example).

Three questions only:

What worked well this week?

What felt hard or unfair?

What is one thing we'll try different next week?

Example Task

By Week 4, everyone knows:

Phones dock at 10 PM.

Sunday evening = 15-minute reset.

They still roll their eyes. That's fine.
But you notice:

Less arguing at bedtime

Mornings aren't full chaos

You're not chasing everyone with a verbal checklist

Structure becomes the quiet hero.

Small win of Week 4:

"Our home feels just a little lighter and more predictable."

PULLING IT ALL TOGETHER

By Day 30, your child may not be giving you a standing ovation.
They may still:

Test tone

Forget chores

Roll their eyes

But you? You're different.

You're:

Calmer

Clearer

Less available for emotional blackmail

More consistent with your policies

And that changes the entire ecosystem of your home.

Respect doesn't magically appear.
It returns when the climate—tone, expectations, language, systems—supports it.

AUDIT

Be honest with yourself:

Which week does my home need most right now—Tone, Responsibility, Language, or Systems?

Where is respect slipping most consistently—tone, chores, talk-back, phones, or follow-through?

What mindset shift must I make first—

"I can handle their feelings"?

"I deserve help in this house"?

"I am allowed to lead calmly without guilt"?

Pick the week your house needs most and start there, even if you repeat it before moving on.

PRAYER

Lord,
restore respect in our home.

Heal the places where words have wounded.
Soften hard hearts—starting with mine.

Teach us humility, clarity, and compassion.
Give me the courage to lead with consistency,
even when emotions rise.

Guide our hearts as we rebuild what was lost.
Let our home become a place where tone is gentle,

boundaries are clear,
and every person is treated with dignity.

Amen.

TRUTH BOMB

Respect returns when consistency becomes your language.

FINAL SAINT LINE

Thirty days of clarity can reset years of chaos.

CHAPTER FIFTEEN
Raising adults, not dependents

There comes a moment in almost every parent's life when you look at your child — whether they're 13 or 23 — and realize you've been doing a whole lot of extra.

Too much carrying.
Too much reminding.
Too much rescuing.

And one day, something snaps — not in anger, but in clarity.

It's the morning you're washing dishes you didn't dirty, collecting cups that traveled from bedroom to sink like they paid rent, sending reminders you shouldn't have to send, googling solutions for problems that are not yours, and quietly praying:

"Lord, I'm raising a whole adult toddler."

You laugh so you don't cry — because it's uncomfortably true.

This chapter is about that moment.

The realization.
The shift.
The upgrade.

The moment you stop being the household assistant... and start being the household leader.

Because parenting isn't about raising dependents.
It's about raising adults who can stand, think, contribute, and carry their own lives with dignity.

Let's walk into that truth together.

THE OPENING SCENE: THE GRAY-HAIRED TODDLER REVEAL

Let me paint this cinematic masterpiece.

You're in the kitchen.
It's 8 a.m.

The sun is shining.
Birds are singing.
Coffee is brewing.

Here comes your 19-year-old, dragging down the hallway like a confused houseguest.

They open the fridge, stare inside like it might give a TED Talk, and then — without blinking — drop the line that deserves an Oscar:

"Why we ain't got no groceries?"

Saint…

Every ancestor in heaven turned their head at the same time.

You take a breath.
You blink twice.
You respond:

"Because the person who eats them didn't help buy them."

They roll their eyes.
They blow air through their nose like a baby bull.
Then here comes the grand finale:

"I'm grown."

And your whole spirit whispers:

"With whose Wi-Fi?"

This is the moment you realize the truth:
You're dealing with a gray-haired toddler — a grown body with baby habits.

Not because they're incapable.
But because life at home has been too soft, too cushioned, too convenient...
and now the bill has come due.

THE SHIFT: FROM RESCUER TO LEADER

Parents don't create dependence on purpose.
Dependence creeps in quietly.

You answer questions they could Google.

You complete tasks they could do themselves.

You donate your time, peace, and energy until you're emotionally bankrupt.

You cushion every fall because you can't bear to see them struggle.

You fix their crises out of guilt, habit, or fear they'll "hate" you.

And before you know it, you've become:

Uber

Wells Fargo

DoorDash

IT support

Therapist

Personal assistant

And, somehow, the villain

You're carrying their schedule, their feelings, their money, their consequences... all on your back.

But real leadership says:

"If I keep doing it for you, you will never learn to stand."

This chapter is your reset button.

We are not just surviving the gray-haired toddler stage.

We are graduating them — and you — into adulthood.

DEPENDENTS VS. ADULTS: THE CLEAR DIFFERENCE

Let's strip the sugar-coating off and call it what it is.

DEPENDENTS:

Wait to be told

Expect rescue

Avoid responsibility

Live off your calendar, your money, and your energy

Blame you when life gets hard

Want adult privileges with toddler effort

Think "freedom" is a right, not a responsibility

ADULTS:

Take initiative

Manage their own emotions

Contribute at home

Communicate respectfully

Handle consequences without tantrums

Plan ahead

Own their choices

Ask for help, not handouts

Here's the core line:

An adult isn't defined by age — it's defined by accountability.

And accountability is not a personality trait.
It's a skill you teach and a standard you hold.

WHY PARENTS GET STUCK IN THE DEPENDENCY LOOP

Parents don't raise dependents because they're weak.
They raise dependents because they're tender.

Let's tell the truth gently but clearly.

1. Guilt Parenting

"I didn't have much growing up, so I want to give them more."

Beautiful heart. Dangerous strategy.

Giving without teaching doesn't create gratitude — it creates entitlement.

2. Fear of Conflict

"If I set this boundary, they'll explode."
"If I say no, they'll pull away."

So you lower the standard to avoid the smoke.
But silence trains them to believe you owe them softness.

3. Habit

You've been doing everything for so long that it feels normal. They truly believe dishes magically wash themselves and money falls from the sky into your debit card.

Habit is the quiet accomplice of chaos.

4. Rescue Reflex

You solve before they feel discomfort.
You call the school.
You write the email.
You drive the forgotten lunch.
You pay the overdraft fee.

But discomfort is where maturity lives.

5. Misplaced Compassion

You confuse helping with handling.
You say, "I'm just being a good mom/dad,"

but your nervous system is exhausted and their growth is delayed.

TRUTH BOMB:
You cannot keep carrying a child who already has legs.

THE TRANSFORMATION BEGINS WITH ONE QUESTION

Ask yourself — and answer honestly:

"Am I raising an adult… or someone who will need me forever?"

That question stings because it exposes the gap between what you want and what you're allowing.

Here's the good news: you can love deeply
and lead firmly.

You can support
without surrendering your peace.

You can guide
without giving away your entire life.

This chapter is the bridge between:

"I'm tired of this,"
and
"I'm changing this."

THE ADULTING FRAMEWORK: THE BIG FIVE SKILLS EVERY CHILD MUST MASTER

If you want your child to walk into adulthood with confidence instead of chaos, focus here.

These are the Big Five. Not perfection. Not genius. Just baseline competence.

1. Emotional Regulation

If they can't control their emotions, they will struggle to control their decisions.

Teach them to:

Pause before reacting

Use a calm tone

Take breaks when upset (Safe Word Protocol, anyone?)

Identify triggers

Solve problems instead of detonating them

Script:

"Let's talk when your voice is steady. I'm here when you're ready."

You're teaching:

"Big feelings are allowed. Big disrespect is not."

2. Time Management

A child who is never responsible for their own schedule will always be late to life.

Teach:

Calendars and reminders

Setting alarms themselves

Preparing the night before

Owning consequences for lateness

Script:

"Missing the deadline is the consequence — not the punishment."

You are not the human snooze button.

3. Money Boundaries

If they treat your wallet like an ATM, adulthood will humble them quick.

Teach:

Basic budgeting

Saving for wants

Paying for non-essentials

Linking money to work and contribution

Script:

"I only loan money once a year." (Annual Loan Rule)

And when you do help? Vendor only, not "drop cash and hope."

4. Contribution & Chores

Chores aren't just about a clean house.
They're about training the muscle of contribution.

Teach:

Weekly responsibilities that matter

Shared ownership of the home

Pride in finished tasks

Script:

"Everyone who lives here contributes here."

Not as punishment — as preparation.

5. Communication & Respect

Respect is the passport that travels everywhere: school, work, relationships, the law.

Teach:

Clear, direct speech

Looking people in the eye

The 10-word sentence (short, clear, no drama)

"Try again with respect"

Tone awareness

Script:

"Respect is the entry fee for this conversation."

TRUTH BOMB:
Your home is the training ground for the world.

THE MOMENT YOU STOP RESCUING — THEY START RISING

The biggest upgrade you can make as a parent?

Stop solving problems your child is old enough to solve.

Some examples:

"Mom, can you call the school?"

"No, sweetheart. You're capable. Call them and let me know how it goes."

"Dad, I don't know how to fill this out."

"Read it carefully, do your best, and then bring me your questions."

"Can you bring me lunch? I forgot."

"No baby. Adults prepare. What will you do differently tomorrow?"

"Can I borrow money till Friday?"

"What's your plan? Show me your budget and how you'll pay it back."

You're not being mean.
You're refusing to be their permanent Plan A, B, C, and D.

TRUTH BOMB:
When you protect them from consequences, you also protect them from growth.

THE SYSTEM: HOW TO SHIFT YOUR CHILD FROM DEPENDENT TO ADULT

You don't need a 97-step master plan.
You need a simple, repeatable system.

Four steps. Clean. Simple. Sustainable.

STEP 1 — Step Back Without Abandoning

You don't disappear.
You just stop micromanaging.

You coach, you don't carry.

You support; you don't supply everything.

You guide; you don't grab the wheel.

Script:

"I'm here to support you, not to carry you."

STEP 2 — Require Participation

Every privilege is tied to contribution.

Wi-Fi, rides, spending money, car keys, time in your house... all linked to effort.

"Live here = contribute here."

Script:

"In this home, privileges follow participation."

This is how you shift from "They're doing me a favor" energy to "We're a team" reality.

STEP 3 — Let Natural Consequences Teach What Lectures Cannot

You don't have to invent creative punishments.
Life is an excellent teacher.

If they:

Don't wake up → They're late.

Don't study → They fail.

Don't budget → They're broke until the next pay.

Don't clean → They live in the mess they created.

You can empathize without erasing the consequence:

"That's tough. I know it doesn't feel good. What's your plan so this doesn't happen again?"

Natural consequences are not cruelty.
They're curriculum.

STEP 4 — Praise Effort, Not Dependency

Don't just celebrate As and trophies.
Celebrate adulting moves: initiative, honesty, effort, problem-solving.

"I noticed you handled that bank call by yourself."

"You apologized without me prompting you. That's grown."

"You budgeted your own money this month. I'm proud of you."

Script:

"You handled that like an adult. That's the direction we're going."

You're feeding the identity you want to see multiplied.

REALITY CHECK: WHEN A CHILD MEETS THE WORLD

Here's a scene you'll recognize sooner or later.

Your adult child gets their first real job.

Day 1 — they're excited.
Day 3 — they're annoyed.
Day 7 — they stomp in the door ready to testify:

"The manager was talking to me crazy.
She got an attitude.
She doesn't like me."

You sip your tea because you already know:
Respect travels… or it doesn't.

Calmly, you ask:

"Did you arrive on time?"

"Did you follow instructions?"

"How was your tone?"

"Did you try again with respect?"

You're not throwing them under the bus.
You're holding up the mirror:

"Adulting is not just about what people do to you — it's about how you show up."

That job is prepping them for the world in ways home never could.
And that's the point.

WHEN YOUR CHILD SAYS "I'M GROWN" — HERE'S THE SCRIPT

At some point, they will puff their chest and announce:

"I'm grown."

Take a deep breath, and try this:

"Being grown is not a feeling — it's a function.
If you want adult freedom, you must show adult responsibility."

That's it. That's the sermon.
You can go back to your coffee.

MINI TRUTH BOMBS — CHAPTER 15 EDITION

Adulthood isn't given — it's demonstrated.
If you do it for them, they'll wait for you forever.
Comfort creates dependents. Structure creates adults.

REFLECT & RESET

What responsibilities am I currently carrying that my child should handle?

Be specific: laundry, emails, scheduling, wake-ups, money.

What fear keeps me rescuing instead of leading?

Fear they'll fail?

Fear they'll be mad?

Fear they'll pull away?

What is ONE adulting skill my child must develop this month?

Budgeting?

Waking up on time?

Calling places on their own?

Managing school or work deadlines?

Today's Tweak:

Choose one task you will stop doing for your child — and let them rise.

AUDIT

Am I parenting for their comfort or their maturity?

Where do I still act like their permanent Plan B, C, and D?

What will change in the next year if I keep rescuing at this level?

What will change if I stop?

PRAYER

Lord,
help me raise adults, not dependents.

Show me where I am over-carrying what my child needs to learn to carry.
Give me courage to step back without stepping away.

Heal the guilt that keeps me rescuing.
Steady the fear that keeps me from setting firm boundaries.

Teach my child responsibility, resilience, and respect —
and teach me to trust the seeds I have already planted.

Let our home become a training ground for adulthood,
not a shelter from every consequence.

Give me wisdom to support without surrender,
and strength to love without losing myself.

Amen.

TRUTH BOMB

Raising adults means you stop doing for them what they are fully capable of doing for themselves.

FINAL SAINT LINE

Raise the adult you want them to become — not the dependent they're used to being.

CHAPTER SIXTEEN
When the world pushes back

You can love your child with your whole heart...

...but the world?

The world does not care who carried them for nine months,
who sat up all night with fevers,
who bent over backwards to give them a good life.

The world responds to behavior, not backstory.

And when a child's respect at home slips, life simply finishes the lesson you started.

This is that truth-telling chapter.
The one no parent *wants* to read—
but every parent is secretly relieved to *understand*.

Because once you see how respect (or the lack of it) shows up outside your walls, you realize something vital:

Home is the training ground.
The world is the exam.

So let's go where your child will eventually go:

The school office

The college inbox

The first job

The roommate contract

The mentor meeting

The hallway you never want to see: the court corridor

This is where the gray-haired toddler finally meets gravity.

And baby…
gravity wins every time.

Scene One: The School Visit Nobody Wants

Picture this.

A high school senior walks into the principal's office like he's walking into his mama's kitchen—
no urgency, no apology, no respect.

He's already been warned about his tone with teachers.
Already been told that skipping assignments doesn't erase deadlines.
Already been coached about showing up late.

But today he crosses a new line.
He tells a teacher:

"You can wait."

At home, maybe he gets away with that.
Maybe you sigh.

Maybe you snap and then let it go because you're tired, busy, or just don't have the emotional energy to debate tone before coffee.

But the teacher?

The teacher is not built like that.

Within 30 minutes, his mama is sitting in a metal chair in an office that smells like paper, stress, and peppermint gum while the principal reads infractions like they're going line-by-line through a W-2.

The mother is stunned.

"Wait... he said WHAT to you?"

The teacher is stunned that she's stunned.

And the student?

Unbothered.
Because the habits learned in the kitchen just showed up in the classroom—louder, sharper, and with witnesses.

Respect travels.

Disrespect travels faster.

TRUTH BOMB:
What you let slide at home is what the world will step on.

Scene Two: College Doesn't Coddle

Now take that same home training and drop it in a college professor's inbox.

A freshman fires off an email at 2:37 a.m.:

"Hey, I need an extension. Something came up."

No greeting.
No explanation.
No accountability.
No respect.

At 8:01 a.m., the professor responds:

"Request denied.
Syllabus policy applies to all students."

The freshman is shocked.
Offended.
Ready to call you crying.

Because at home, "something came up" might work.
But college is not home.

College is not concerned with:

Their mood

Their excuses

Their late-night feelings

College is a training ground for adulthood.

In college:

Office hours end at 4, not "whenever you feel ready"

Professors do not take being yelled at

Extensions are earned, not demanded

Accountability is baked into the culture

Your child can be brilliant and still hit a wall if they never learned to respect time, tone, and policy.

TRUTH BOMB:
College is where excuses go to die.

Scene Three: The Job That Didn't Care

Your teen lands their first job—Chick-fil-A, Target, UPS, the mall, wherever.

Day 1: they're excited.
Day 3: they're irritated.
Day 7: they're late.

Not two hours late.
Just late enough to send one message:

"The rules don't really apply to me."

They show up fifteen minutes behind, three times in two weeks.

When the supervisor pulls them aside, they get attitude:

"Ugh, I was only fifteen minutes late."

Only.

To a payroll system?
To a manager with six people out?
To a store depending on shift coverage?

There is no *only*.

Two warnings later, they get terminated.
They come home and say:

"They just didn't like me."

No, baby.

They didn't like:

Being short-staffed

Having to rearrange coverage

Carrying someone who didn't carry their weight

Just like you don't like it when chores don't get done at home.

That termination isn't cruelty.

It's curriculum.

The world teaches with consequences, not conversations.

TRUTH BOMB:
A boss is not raising your child. They are managing your child. There's a difference.

Scene Four: The Roommate Reality Check

A messy teen at home becomes a messy roommate in freshman housing.

The disrespectful tone at home becomes roommate conflict by Week 2.

The "It's not that serious" attitude becomes a quiet-hours violation.

The habit of leaving dishes "for later" becomes a nasty kitchen nobody wants to use.

Your child thinks their roommate is "doing too much."
But the roommate was never trained to tolerate their chaos.

A roommate will not:

Clean up after them

Chase them for rent

Tolerate stolen food

Accept slammed doors

Babysit their moods

They will simply:

File a complaint

Get reassigned

Or move out

And suddenly your child finds out:

"Oh... my habits affect other people."

TRUTH BOMB:
The roommate phase is where gray-haired toddlers get evicted from their own habits.

Scene Five: Law Enforcement Doesn't Negotiate Feelings

This is the section nobody wants, but everybody needs.

Disrespect at home becomes disrespect in public.
Disrespect in public becomes resistance.
Resistance becomes escalation.
Escalation becomes danger.

Police do not read backstory.
They read:

Body language

Volume

Compliance

Movement

Tone

They are not interpreting the moment like a parent.
They are interpreting risk.

One unnecessary attitude moment can change a life trajectory.

You can train respect gently at home...
or the world will train it loudly outside.

TRUTH BOMB:
Teach respect early so your child survives reality later.

Scene Six: When Opportunity Watches Their Attitude

Your child finally gets an internship with a family friend.
A connection you prayed for.

But they show up:

Texting mid-conversation

Mumbling

Avoiding eye contact

Rolling eyes

Half-doing the work

Acting bored and entitled

Suddenly, the opportunity dries up.

Not because they weren't capable.
Because respect wasn't portable.

In most fields, mentors do not have time to correct basic respect.
They simply close the door quietly and move on to the next kid in line.

TRUTH BOMB:
Opportunities travel on respect. Doors close on attitude.

Why the World Pushes Back So Hard

Because adulthood is built on:

Respect

Accountability

Timeliness

Tone

Responsibility

Follow-through

Self-awareness

Emotional regulation

The world is not "out to get your child."
The world is neutral.

It simply gives back the same energy your child sends out.

At home, you can buffer the impact:

You call the teacher

You email the professor

You explain to the boss

You smooth things over

But outside?

There is no buffer.
No cushion.
No soft landing.

Which means your home cannot just be a place of comfort. It has to be a practice field.

TRUTH BOMB:
Home is the practice field. The world is the game.

How to Prepare Your Child Before the World Does

Let's get practical. This isn't about scaring your child.
It's about preparing them.

1. Use Real-World Scripts at Home

Instead of:

"Don't talk to me like that."

Try:

"If you use that tone in the world, here's exactly what happens—a teacher writes you up, a boss sends you home, or a cop sees you as a threat."

Connect home behavior to real-world outcomes.

2. Bring School/Work Language Into Your House

Normalize lines like:

"Deadlines matter."

"Tone affects access."

"Respect earns opportunity."

"Accountability is part of adulthood."

These aren't corporate slogans.
They're survival skills.

3. Create a Weekly "Respect Travels" Check-In

Once a week, ask:

"Where did respect show up this week—for you or someone else?"

"Where did disrespect show up?"

"What did you learn from what you saw?"

Keep it short, not a lecture—just a family reality check.

4. Require One "Respect Challenge" a Week

Give them one simple respect rep to practice:

Speak clearly to an adult (no mumbling)

Ask a question in class or at work

Send a polite email to a teacher/coach

Offer help at home or work without being asked

Practice "Try again with respect" when their tone slips

You are building muscle memory for real life.

5. Practice "Try Again" Culture

When the tone is off, you don't just say, "Don't talk to me like that."

You say:

"Try that again with respect."

Then you give them a chance to repeat the sentence the right way.

Not because they're being punished—
because they're training.

6. Model Respect Under Pressure

Your child is always watching how *you* talk to:

Customer service

Teachers

Waiters

Cashiers

Neighbors

Other drivers

If you want respect to travel out of your house, it has to live inside your house—even when you're tired, stressed, or irritated.

You won't be perfect. That's okay.
When you mess it up, you model repair:

"I shouldn't have spoken like that. Let me try again."

That's respect that travels.

MINI TRUTH BOMBS

Respect is a passport. Tone is TSA.
The world rewards emotional adults, not emotional toddlers.
Your child can be talented and still lose opportunities if they can't manage their mouth.
Disrespect at home is rehearsal. Disrespect in public is the performance.

REFLECT & RESET

Which real-world consequence is my child most at risk for right now?

School write-ups?

Job loss?

College fallout?

Roommate drama?

Police escalation?

What habit at home is preparing my child for the wrong outcome?

You laughing off disrespect?

You rescuing them from every late assignment?

You arguing with teachers instead of correcting your child?

You letting slamming, yelling, or eye-rolling slide?

What is ONE script or standard I can introduce this week to teach respect that travels?

"Try again with respect."

"Respect is your passport—use it."

"You can be upset. You still must be respectful."

Today's Tweak:
Pick one area—tone, time, or follow-through—and start treating home like the training ground, not the exception.

Where have I unintentionally protected my child from consequences that would have taught them respect?

Where am I minimizing behavior at home that would be a big problem in the real world?

What system (policy, script, or consequence) do I need to put in place so respect becomes a daily habit, not a special occasion?

PRAYER

Lord,

Help me see clearly where my child's habits are leading them.
Give me courage to train respect at home
instead of waiting for the world to do it for me.

Show me how to connect love with truth,
comfort with correction,
and home with preparation.

Protect my child in the places I cannot go.
Prepare them for rooms I will never see.

Teach them to carry respect in their tone,
in their choices,
in their friendships,

in their work,
and in every space where their name will travel.

Make our home a practice field where they learn
that honor, responsibility, and self-control
are not optional—they are survival.

In Jesus' name,
Amen.

TRUTH BOMB

**Teach respect at home,
so the world doesn't become their first real teacher.**

FINAL SAINT LINE

**Teach respect at home—
so when the world pushes back, they're ready to stand.**

CHAPTER SEVENTEEN
The discipline pivot: parenting with consequences that actually teach

There comes a moment in every parent's life when you realize:

You aren't disciplining anymore — you're just talking.

Talking loud.
Talking long.
Talking in circles.
Talking into the void like a motivational speaker at a family reunion nobody asked for.

And nothing changes.

That's the breaking point for most parents — the moment you whisper to yourself:

"Something has to give, and that something might be... me."

Not *you* as a person.
Not your love.
Not your authority.

But the way you've been enforcing consequences — or avoiding them — because deep down, you've been praying your child would just magically "get it together" if you explained it one more time, one more way, on one more late night.

Saint, if you only parent from your throat (lectures, threats, repeating yourself), you'll stay tired and hoarse.

If you parent from your policies, you'll finally breathe.

This chapter is the pivot point — the moment you stop trying to scare, beg, shame, or sermon your child into better behavior... and you step into calm, steady leadership that:

Teaches instead of traumatizes

Corrects instead of crushes

Guides instead of guilt-tripping

This is the grown-up discipline your home has been waiting for.

The Discipline Myth That's Been Playing You

Most of us grew up believing discipline meant punishment.

We heard:

"Do this or else."

"Because I said so."

"Wait until we get home."

"You ain't gon' be satisfied until I lose my mind."

So we learned: discipline = fear.

But here's the truth:

Punishment is reactive.

Discipline is instructional.

Punishment says:

"Feel bad."

Discipline says:

"Learn something."

Punishment is about control.
Discipline is about development.

Punishment triggers fear.
Discipline builds respect.

Punishment can shut a child down.
Discipline trains them to rise up.

Here's the TRUTH BOMB most households never write on the fridge:

Discipline without teaching is just noise.

And parents are exhausted because they're running a noise factory instead of a training center.

Why Your Old Discipline System Stopped Working

Look, your child isn't three anymore.

Their:

Brain

Attitude

Tone

Hormones

Height

Vocabulary

all got upgrades — but your discipline system stayed in 2009.

That's like trying to run TikTok on a flip phone.

Kids today do not respond to:

Long speeches

Empty threats

Inconsistent rules

Consequences that don't match the behavior

Parents who yell but never follow through

Your child is not confused.
They're conditioned.

If the consequence is:

Unpredictable

Emotional

Inconsistent

...they adjust their behavior to you, not to the rule.

A household without predictable discipline becomes a circus with invisible clowns — everyone performing, nobody learning.

The Discipline Pivot Starts With You

Before we get into scripts, systems, and consequences that actually *land*, we have to check the foundation.

You can't build healthy discipline on an unstable parent.

Ask yourself:

"Am I parenting from reaction... or intention?"

Emotional discipline begins with emotional sobriety (Chapter 13).
Now we take that sobriety and build structure around it — a

discipline plan that runs the house even when your feelings don't.

Here's the pivot:

Old Parenting:
You break a rule → I lose my mind → both of us get headaches

New Parenting:
You break a rule → the system responds → I stay calm → you learn

See the difference?

Discipline isn't about punishment — it's about predictability.

Your child needs consistency more than they need consequences.

The Four Laws of Effective Discipline

These four laws will change your entire household if you let them.

LAW 1 — The Consequence Must Be Related

Messy behavior → cleaning responsibility.
Disrespect → communication reset + privilege pause.
Late curfew → earlier curfew.

Random consequences create resentment.

Relevant consequences create reflection.

LAW 2 — The Consequence Must Be Immediate

Don't wait until Friday to address Wednesday's meltdown.

If your child can't clearly link the behavior to the outcome, they see the consequence as punishment, not teaching.

Immediate = meaningful.

LAW 3 — The Consequence Must Be Consistent

If your child thinks consequences depend on your *mood*, they will learn to manage your mood, not their own behavior.

Consistency is the calm spine of discipline.

LAW 4 — The Consequence Must Be Sustainable

If you can't maintain the consequence for at least a week, don't create it.

You do not need consequences that drain *you*.
You need consequences that train *them*.

Sustainable beats dramatic — every single time.

The Discipline Ladder: Five Levels That Build Grown-Ups

A child should not jump from "warning" to "World War III."

Use the Discipline Ladder — a predictable, step-by-step progression that teaches without escalating.

Level 1 — The Redirect

Low drama. Low energy. Calm voice.

"Try again with respect."

"Pause. Breathe. Start over."

"Let's fix the tone."

This is the first fence.

Most issues stop right here when your consistency is strong.

Level 2 — The Natural Consequence

Let life do some of the teaching.

They slammed the door → they fix the door.

They left the mess → they clean the mess.

They forgot the assignment → they face the late grade.

Natural consequences build maturity without long lectures.

Level 3 — The Logical Consequence

Behavior → related impact.

Disrespect → loss of phone during communication time (calls/texts), not for random punishment.

Missed chores → complete the chore plus one bonus task.

Breaking curfew → temporarily earlier curfew.

Logical consequences say:

"Your choices shape your access."

Level 4 — The Privilege Pause

Notice — not revenge.

Phones, rides, outings, Wi-Fi, streaming, sleepovers — all privileges, not rights.

Pausing a privilege sends the message:

"Responsibility comes before reward."

You're not destroying their life.
You're aligning their lifestyle with their level of maturity.

Level 5 — The System Reset

Use this when the pattern is bigger than a single incident.

When:

Disrespect becomes culture

Defiance becomes language

Chaos becomes normal

...it's time to reset the entire system:

Curfews tighten

Chores increase

Access decreases

Expectations rise

This is not a tantrum from the parent.

It's a recalibration of the home.

How to Enforce Consequences Without Losing Your Mind

Here's where your Calm Spine shines.

Rule #1 — One Sentence Only

Over-explaining kills your authority.

Aim for a 7–10-word sentence:

"Phone is paused until respect returns."

"Curfew resets this weekend. Try again next week."

"Chores first. Privileges after. That's the policy."

Clean. Clear. Done.

Rule #2 — No Back-and-Forth

Your boundary is not a debate table.

Child: "That's not fair!"
You: "We can discuss it tomorrow."

Child: "Why are you doing this?"
You: "This is the rule today."

They can be upset.
You don't have to be *persuaded*.

Rule #3 — No Emotional Matching

Their volume is not your cue.
Their eye roll is not your marching orders.

You maintain calm — because calm is power.

Rule #4 — Consequence Ends on a Win

When they show growth — even a small step — release the consequence with encouragement:

"You handled that well. I see your effort."

This teaches them:

"Respect restores access."

Discipline becomes a bridge back to connection, not a wall that stays forever.

Three Discipline Scripts Every Parent Needs

You don't need 47 monologues.
You need three solid anchors.

Script 1 — The Calm Reset

"Pause. Let's reset the tone."

Short. Neutral. Teaches emotional regulation.

Script 2 — The Boundary Reminder

"This is the rule. We'll revisit later."

Stops negotiations instantly.

Script 3 — The Privilege Pause

"We'll pause the privilege. You can try again tomorrow."

Not punishment.
Practice.

Case Study: The Teen Who Thought She Was a Roommate

A mom told me:

"My daughter walks in and out like she's paying rent."

No greeting.
No chores.
No curfew accountability.
No contribution.

Just vibes.

The pivot? A simple, calm system:

One weekly chore (non-negotiable)

Curfew set and tracked

Phone docking at 9 p.m.

One privilege paused when disrespect entered the room

No screaming.
No name-calling.
No "I do everything for you" speeches.

Within three weeks:

Tone shifted

Behavior improved

The relationship softened

Not because Mom yelled louder —
but because she finally got consistent.

Case Study: The 10-Year-Old Who Weaponized Tears

This child cried to escape consequences.

Any correction → instant meltdown → parent backed down.

We introduced the Calm Spine Script:

"I hear that you're upset. The consequence still stands."

No sarcasm.
No shaming.
Just steady.

Within 10 days, the tears still came…
but the behavior changed.

Because manipulation stopped working.

Kids rise when parents stop folding.

The Secret Discipline Tool: Future Focus

Instead of:

"Why did you do that?!"

Use:

"What's your plan for next time?"

You can still address what happened, but you end in the future.

Discipline that looks forward creates growth.

Discipline that stays backward creates shame.

You are raising a future adult, not auditioning a perfect child.

MINI TRUTH BOMBS

A consequence delivered calmly teaches twice — once through the boundary, once through your tone.

If the system changes daily, your child won't change at all.

Consistency is the real discipline — not the consequence itself.

REFLECT & RESET

Where do I over-explain instead of enforcing?

Which consequence is hardest for me to maintain consistently?

Where am I parenting from my feelings instead of from clear policy?

What is one discipline system I can commit to for the next 7 days?

ACTION STEP: The Discipline Pivot Plan

Choose one area to apply this system for 7 days:

Tone

Chores

Curfew

Phone/Wi-Fi

Disrespect patterns

Pick one.
Write the policy in one sentence.
Decide the consequence before the conflict.
Hold the line — calmly — for a full week.

Then watch what shifts:
in them,
and in you.

AUDIT

Do my children know the rules *and* the consequences — clearly?

Do my consequences match the behavior, or are they random and emotional?

Am I more committed to peace-and-quiet in the moment, or growth in the long run?

PRAYER

Lord,

Teach me how to discipline with wisdom, not wrath.
Help me trade yelling for clarity,
threats for steady follow-through,
and fear-based punishment for growth-based guidance.

Show me the places where my inconsistency is confusing my child.
Give me the courage to hold the line
even when they don't like it,
and the tenderness to reconnect
when the consequence has done its job.

Let my tone be calm,
my boundaries be clear,
and my heart stay soft
while my spine stays strong.

In Jesus' name,
Amen.

TRUTH BOMB

Discipline isn't the storm — discipline is the shelter that keeps everyone safe.

FINAL SAINT LINE

Discipline isn't the storm — it's the shelter. Step inside and lead

CHAPTER EIGHTEEN
The annual family reset meeting: bringing order back to the house you built

Every healthy home needs a moment when everybody stops, sits down, and remembers who we are and how we live here.

Not in crisis.
Not in chaos.
Not when somebody's shoe is already flying across the room like a discount Broadway musical.

A reset — a deliberate pause — is one of the most underrated parenting tools on earth.

And yet, most families have never had a real one.

Most households run on:

Unwritten rules

Old emotional habits

"We've just always done it this way"

Then one disrespectful season hits, everybody's irritated, the energy in the home starts dropping like a tired Wi-Fi signal... and we wonder why:

The kids are wild

The adults are exhausted

Even the dog is looking for new housing options

The Annual Family Reset Meeting is how you stop the free-fall.

This chapter gives you the script, the structure, and the leadership energy to re-center your home — calmly, kindly, and with a spine made of titanium.

Hear me clearly:

A family that never resets becomes a family that never respects.

Welcome to the meeting that changes that.

THE HOOK — Why You Need This Meeting (Even If You Think You Don't)

Families drift.
Roles shift.
Boundaries blur.
Expectations expire.

And the truth is: no one holds a house accountable unless the leader calls a meeting.

A reset meeting is not punishment — it's maintenance.

Think of it like changing the oil in your car. If you avoid it, small problems turn into expensive disasters.

But with a little structure, a little clarity, and a little accountability?

Your home starts breathing again.

Kids behave differently when the adults show up differently.

Adults show up differently when the plan is simple, predictable, and repeated every single year.

So let's build your blueprint.

THE PURPOSE — What This Meeting Does

The Annual Family Reset Meeting has three core goals:

1. Reestablish Clarity

Everyone knows:

The rules

The routines

The expectations

What happens when those are ignored

Confusion is the enemy of respect.

2. Strengthen Connection

Because:

Discipline without connection feels like control.

Connection without discipline feels like chaos.

This meeting balances both.

3. Restore Respect

Respect does not grow in fog.
Respect grows in structure.

You're about to give your family the structure they didn't even know they were craving.

THE ENERGY — How You Enter the Meeting

You are not:

The judge

The detective

The tired parent begging these children to stop acting like they were raised by community guidelines

No.

You walk in like a CEO hosting a quarterly review: calm, friendly, clear, and unbothered.

Your tone sets the tone.

If you're defensive, they'll get defensive.

If you're frantic, they'll shut down.

If you're calm, they'll get curious.

Before the meeting, take ten deep breaths and repeat my favorite line:

"I am confident in your ability to figure it out for yourself."

Say it until your nervous system believes you.

Then begin.

THE STRUCTURE — The Angela Saint Reset Meeting Blueprint

Use this exactly as written the first time. You can tweak later but start here. It works because it's predictable, repeatable, and calm.

PHASE 1 — The Welcome (2 minutes)

Script:

"Family, thank you for being here. Today is our Annual Reset Meeting — a time where we pause, realign, and make sure our home is a place of peace, respect, and teamwork. This is not a punishment. This is maintenance."

Tone: soft but firm — organized compassion.

Goal: Get everyone listening without flinching.

PHASE 2 — The Wins (3 minutes)

Why it works: Kids (and adults) behave better when they feel seen for more than their mistakes.

Say:

"Before we talk about anything else, I want us to name a few wins from this year. Something each of us did well, improved, or handled with maturity."

You can go around the room or name a few you've noticed:

"I saw you really stepping up with your little brother."

"You handled that school situation with a lot of maturity."

"We all got through a hard season together."

This moment lowers defenses.
It also teaches them that accountability starts with gratitude, not accusation.

PHASE 3 — The House Standards (5 minutes)

This is where you restate — not debate — the baseline rules of the home.

Three to five standards maximum. Short, simple, non-negotiable.

Examples (PG-friendly):

Speak respectfully.

Complete your responsibilities before leisure.

Keep common spaces clean.

Honor bedtime and morning routines.

Speak to your parents with clarity, not chaos.

You might say:

"These are our house standards. They apply to all of us, every day. We will come back to these when we make decisions and when there's conflict."

TRUTH BOMB:

A home without standards becomes a home without peace.

Say it gently but say it.

PHASE 4 — The Consequence Framework (3 minutes)

Clarity is kindness.

Script:

"When a standard is ignored, the consequence is automatic. Not emotional. Not personal. Predictable."

Give 3–4 examples:

Loss of phone access for 24 hours

Chore swap (you get an extra chore; someone else gets a break)

Early bedtime

No rides for 48 hours

Quiet hour in your room

The rule: A consequence must be keepable.

If you can't enforce it calmly, it's not a consequence — it's a threat.

You're not performing discipline for effect. You're setting policies you can actually live with.

PHASE 5 — The Family Calendar (5 minutes)

This step saves parents YEARS of stress.

You review the rhythms that tend to cause the most conflict:

Chores and who owns what

School schedules and major projects

Work schedules

Curfews and check-in times

Tech boundaries (phone docking, Wi-Fi cut-off)

Weekly family reset (a quick check-in)

Any upcoming transitions (new job, new school, sports season, travel)

This one step cuts down the number-one cause of family drama:

"I didn't know."

After this meeting, they know.

PHASE 6 — The Respect Pledge (2 minutes)

This is where everyone speaks a single sentence of commitment.

Examples:

"I will speak with more kindness."

"I will handle my responsibilities without being asked twice."

"I will manage my tone, even when I'm upset."

"I will ask for help respectfully."

"I will follow the tech and curfew rules without arguing."

Parents go first.

You model that this is a shared responsibility, not just a "kids, get it together" speech.

This creates ownership without turning the home into a courtroom.

PHASE 7 — The Closing (1 minute)

Keep it short. This is not the altar call at a four-hour revival.

Script:

"Thank you for being here. I'm proud of us. We move forward from this moment with clarity and a fresh start."

Then stop.

Close the meeting. Hug, high-five, or dismiss — whatever fits your family culture.

We are not doing filibusters in the living room.

WHAT TO EXPECT AFTER THE MEETING

Expect a shift — not perfection.

Some kids will test the new structure on Day 1.

Why?

Because they need to know if you mean it.

That's not rebellion — that's research.

Hold the line calmly.

You are not fighting your child.
You are fighting the pattern.

Within a week or two, the energy in your home will start to feel:

Lighter

Calmer

More predictable

Kids thrive in stability.
Adults thrive in peace.

A reset meeting gives both.

WHEN TO HOLD THE NEXT ONE

Once a year. Non-negotiable.

Good times, hard times, graduation years, quiet years — it doesn't matter. Your family still needs a yearly reset.

But if the household starts spiraling mid-year?

Host a Quarterly Mini Reset

Ten minutes. Three agenda items:

One win

One problem

One solution

No drama.
No monologues.
Just adjustments.

This is what leadership looks like.

MINI TRUTH BOMBS FOR CHAPTER 18

Respect grows where clarity lives.
Your leadership sets the emotional thermostat of your home.

A meeting is not a lecture — it's a reset.

Peace is not an accident. It's a practice.

REFLECT & RESET

What is one standard my home needs to reestablish right now?

How can I bring calm leadership into our next family conversation?

What old habit must I release to make space for a healthier household rhythm?

FINAL SAINT LINE

When a family knows the plan, peace knows the way home.

CHAPTER NINETEEN
When your child blames you for everything: the art of standing tall without breaking yourself

If you parent long enough, you'll eventually hear it:

"This is all your fault."

Sometimes it's whispered.
Sometimes it's shouted.
Sometimes it's delivered with tears, slammed doors, and an attitude that could power a small city.

You'll get blamed for:

The bad grade

The breakup

The mess they made

The job they lost

The fact that there are "no snacks in this house" except raisins

Blame is a language kids learn early and perfect over time.

Some wield it like a shield.
Some use it like a weapon.
Some throw it around because they don't yet have the maturity to hold their own consequences.

And the parent — tired, loving, human — becomes the nearest target.

Let's put truth on the table:

Being blamed for everything is not the same as being responsible for everything.

But when you're exhausted or already carrying quiet guilt, the lines blur. You start wondering:

Did I do something wrong?

Am I ruining my child?

Is this my fault?

No, Saint.

You're not ruining your child — you're raising one.

And raising humans means bumping into their projections, their pain, and the stories they tell themselves to avoid hard truths.

This chapter is about how to step out of the blame battlefield and into calm, mature leadership — without collapsing, over-explaining, or swallowing lies that were never yours to carry.

THE HOOK — Blame Is a Mirror, Not a Verdict

Kids blame parents for one big reason:

They don't yet know how to process their own discomfort.

Blame is a shortcut.
A fast escape.
A way to avoid:

Effort

Consequences

Accountability

Self-reflection

Emotional maturity

Here's the part nobody told you:

When a child blames you, they're revealing their capacity, not your failure.

Blame says nothing about your worth.
It says a lot about their readiness.

Your job isn't to win the argument or cross-examine their feelings.

Your job is to model leadership that invites growth.

WHY BLAME HURTS SO MUCH

Blame hits the soft places.

It pokes the guilt you've carried for years.
It scrapes over old parent-wounds and whispers:

"See? You're just like them. You're messing up too."

That's why this chapter matters.

When your child blames you, it is not the time to collapse. It's the time to stand still, breathe deeply, and let the storm pass around you instead of through you.

This is emotional adulthood — the exact skill you want your child to learn.

You don't teach it by reacting.
You teach it by demonstrating it.

THE BLAME PLAYBOOK — 5 COMMON PATTERNS (AND HOW TO NEUTRALIZE THEM)

Blame has patterns. Once you see them, you stop taking them personally and start responding on purpose.

1. The Rewrite Artist

Lines you'll hear:

"You never helped me."

"You always yell."

"You don't care about me."

"You were never there for me."

They take one moment, stretch it over ten years, and hit "repeat" like it's a playlist.

Your Script:

"I hear you're upset. Let's talk about this when we can both use the real version of the story."

Not sarcastic. Not petty. Just clear.

You're saying:
We can deal in truth, not dramatized reruns.

TRUTH BOMB:
Don't fight the rewrite — calmly return to reality.

2. The Deflector

Every time you try to address a behavior, they dodge.

You: "Why weren't the dishes done?"
Child: "Well, if you hadn't cooked so much, there wouldn't be so many dishes."

You: "You missed curfew."
Child: "You didn't remind me what time to be home."

The goal is simple: if they can keep you on defense, they never have to look at themselves.

Your Script:

"The question still stands. Why weren't the dishes done?"

or

"The curfew was clear. What happened with your choice?"

Short. Clean. On-topic.

You are not chasing their deflection down twelve side streets.

3. The Historian

They dig up something you did ten years ago and lay it at your feet like Exhibit A.

Child:
"You yelled at me when I was 9! That's why I don't listen now!"

Is there truth that you've grown since then? Yes.
Is that the reason they skipped class last week? No.

Your Script:

"I'm open to healing the past. And I'm willing to own where I've grown. But today's responsibility still belongs to you."

You don't deny the past.
You just refuse to let it erase today's accountability.

TRUTH BOMB:
History can explain behavior. It does not excuse it.

4. The Victim Narrator

In this story, everything happens to them.
Nothing happens because of them.

The teacher had it out for them

The boss "was trippin'"

Every friend is "fake"

Every problem is "somebody else"

They want rescue. They want a co-signer.

Your Script:

"I'm sorry this feels hard. What's one step you can take to move forward?"

They reach for a savior.
You hand them a strategy.

5. The Emotional Bulldozer

When all else fails, they push harder with volume, tears, or attitude.

If they can flood your nervous system, they can shut down the conversation.

Voices rise

Tears fall

Doors slam

Words get sharp

Suddenly the original issue disappears, and now the whole house is dealing with the fallout.

Your Script:

"I'm willing to talk when our tones are calm. Let's pause here."

You're not punishing them.
You're teaching emotional regulation and protecting your own peace.

THE CALM SPINE FRAMEWORK — HOW TO HOLD YOURSELF WHEN YOU'RE BEING BLAMED

You cannot control their words.
You can absolutely control your stance.

1. Name What's Happening (Inside Yourself)

Silently tell yourself:

"This is blame. Not truth."

That one internal sentence keeps you from swallowing every word like a diagnosis.

2. Slow Your Breathing

Not dramatic. Just steady.

Inhale slowly through your nose

Exhale a beat longer through your mouth

Drop your shoulders

Kids match the respiratory rate of the adult in the room.
Your breath is a boundary.

3. Shift From Defending to Leading

You are not on trial.

You don't need to present:

Exhibit A (your sacrifices)

Exhibit B (your bank account)

Exhibit C (your childhood trauma)

You simply shift to leadership:

"What part of this do you want to take responsibility for today?"

Now the spotlight moves.
Not to shame them, but to invite adulthood.

4. Use the Two-Question Rule

When blame runs in circles, you put it in a box:

What have you tried?

What's your plan?

If they've tried nothing, that's clarity.
If they have no plan, that's clarity too.

Either way, you're out of the emotional tornado and back in reality.

5. End the Conversation When the Tone Goes Left

Not in rage. In self-respect.

Your Script:

"I won't continue this conversation in blame. We can talk again when we're calmer."

Then you step away.

No stomping.
No dramatic exits.
Just a quiet, powerful no more.

WHY YOU MUST STOP OVER-EXPLAINING

Kids who lean on blame often expect a full PowerPoint presentation every time they're upset:

You bring:

Context

Your heart

Your intentions

Your receipts

Your tears

They bring:

"Still your fault."

When you over-explain, you accidentally teach this dangerous lesson:

"If your feelings are strong enough, my worth is negotiable."

Absolutely not.

Your new mantra:

"I explain once. I stand twice."

Short explanations. Long consistency.

SCENES FROM REAL HOMES — AND THE RESET SCRIPTS

Scene 1 — The Teen Who Failed a Class

Teen:
"If you hadn't stressed me out all year, I would've passed!"

Old pattern:
You panic, defend, and replay every decision you've ever made.

New pattern:

"I hear your frustration. But the grade is yours. Let's talk about your plan for recovery."

You validate the feeling without accepting the fiction.

Scene 2 — The Grown Child Who Comes Home Broke

Adult child:
"I'm struggling because you never taught me about money!"

Maybe you did.
Maybe you didn't.
Either way, the bills have their name on them now.

Your Script:

"I'm sorry you're feeling overwhelmed. What skill do you want to build next? I'm confident in your ability to figure it out."

You can always grow together.
But you will not carry the full weight of choices you did not make.

Scene 3 — The Adult Looking for a Lifetime Scapegoat

Adult child:
"My relationships fail because of how you raised me!"

Is there room for healing? Yes.
Is their entire adult love life your responsibility? No.

Your Script:

"I'm open to healing conversations, and I'm willing to own where I fell short. But your relationships today belong to you."

You hold space for truth
without surrendering your soul.

THE LEADERSHIP SHIFT — You Are Not the Villain in Their Story

Your child may build a narrative where you are the easy villain.
Why?
Because villains are easier to blame than patterns are to face.

Let them talk.
Let them vent.
Let them feel.

But you do not have to accept every role they assign you.

You funded this story.
You fed them.
You loved them.
You prayed over them.

You are not perfect — but you are not the punching bag of their plot.

Blame dissolves when the adult refuses to dance with it.

THREE HARD TRUTHS PARENTS MUST ACCEPT

1. Your child's feelings are real, but their interpretation might not be.
You can say:
"I believe you feel hurt. I don't agree with the story you're telling about me."

Empathize with the feeling.
Don't endorse the fiction.

2. You can repair the past, but you cannot parent backward.
You can apologize where needed.
You can do better with new information.
But you cannot raise their 8-year-old self again.

Guilt is not a parenting strategy.

3. Blame is often the last stop before growth.
Sometimes blame is just fear wearing loud clothing.
It's easier to say, "You broke me,"
than to whisper, "I need to grow now."

You don't have to rush in and fix that moment.
You just have to stay standing while it passes.

HOW TO EXIT A BLAME CONVERSATION WITH DIGNITY

Use the Saint Exit Line:

"I love you. And I'm confident in your ability to work through this. I'm here when you're ready for a respectful conversation."

You're offering:

Love

Confidence

A boundary

Then you stop.

No extra paragraphs.
No pleading.
No emotional essay.

Just a clear doorway they can walk back through when they're ready to act like the adult they claim to be.

MINI TRUTH BOMBS FOR CHAPTER 19

Blame is the refuge of the unready.
Leadership doesn't defend — it directs.
Your child's version of the story is not the whole story.
You are allowed to exit the blame battlefield.

REFLECT & RESET

What part of my child's blame triggers old guilt in me?

How can I separate their feelings from my actual responsibility?

What script will I use the next time blame shows up at my door?

PRAYER

Lord,
When blame comes loud and heavy,
steady my heart.
Help me listen with compassion
without surrendering to guilt that isn't mine.
Show me what is truly my responsibility
and what belongs to my child to carry.
Teach me to respond with calm, clear leadership
instead of fear, panic, or over-explaining.
Give my child the courage to face their own choices
and the humility to grow beyond blame.
Let our conversations move toward truth,
healing, and mutual respect.
Amen.

FINAL SAINT LINE

When blame knocks, wisdom answers — and peace stays home.

CHAPTER TWENTY
Repair after the storm: how families heal without starting over

Peace doesn't return with an apology.
Respect doesn't return with a hug.

And trust?

Trust returns the same way it was built in the first place—
slowly, intentionally, one brick at a time.

Every home has storms.

Moments when:

Someone says too much

Someone shuts down too fast

Someone raises their voice too high

Someone slams a door and walks away

The real danger isn't the storm itself.
It's what happens after the storm—

whether the house recovers, or

whether the cracks quietly spread.

This chapter is your blueprint for emotional reconstruction.

Not a Hallmark clean slate.
Not a forced forgiveness moment.

Just honest, structured healing that strengthens the family instead of shoving everyone back into the same old patterns.

Because here's the truth every parent has to swallow:

Repair is leadership, not surrender.

What you model during recovery becomes the emotional blueprint your child carries into their:

friendships

relationships

classrooms

workplaces

and their own future home

Let's rebuild the right way.

THE CALM AFTER THE CHAOS: WHY REPAIR MATTERS MORE THAN THE RULES

Most parents secretly believe peace returns when the rule is finally followed.

The phone is turned in

The curfew is honored

The room is clean

The chore is done

But real peace doesn't return when the rule is obeyed.
Real peace returns when the relationship is repaired.

A child can:

follow the rule

finish the chore

say "yes ma'am"

...and still carry:

resentment

shame

confusion

quiet distance from you

So Chapter 20 is your bridge-building chapter.

It teaches your child:

You can make mistakes without losing the people who love you.

You can have conflict without breaking the family.

You can be held accountable and still held with compassion.

You can apologize without being humiliated and forgive without being pressured.

And it teaches you:

You can guide without guilt.

You can correct without cruelty.

You can reconnect without collapsing.

You can lead with softness after you lead with structure.

Repair doesn't erase what happened.
It integrates what happened into something stronger.

Think of a storm-damaged house:
You don't pretend the storm never hit.
You reinforce the beams so it can handle the next one.

That's emotional repair.

And it is one of the greatest gifts you will ever give your child.

THE THREE-STAGE REPAIR MODEL (THE SAINT WAY)

This is your new go-to system after any:

conflict

argument

outburst

boundary push

disrespect moment

Three stages. Same rhythm. Every time.

Stage 1: Reset the Temperature

Before anyone speaks, the emotional thermostat has to drop.

This looks like:

Everyone taking a pause

No one chasing the conversation

No "we're talking about this right now" energy

No guilt speeches

No punishments announced in the heat of anger

You simply set the tone with:

"We'll talk when everyone is calm again."

Calm is the currency of repair.

Without calm, every conversation becomes a remix of the conflict, not a bridge to the solution.

The secret of Stage 1?
Parents must reset first.

Children co-regulate from your energy before they ever regulate from their own maturity.

When you reset, they eventually follow.

Stage 2: Naming Without Blaming

This is the part most families skip.

Instead of processing, they sprint to:

"It's fine."

"Forget it."

"Let's just move on."

Skipping the naming step silently teaches your child:

Feelings don't matter.

We pretend to be okay even when we're not.

Conflict is dangerous, not fixable.

"Moving on" means avoidance, not healing.

So in Stage 2, you speak the truth without weaponizing it.

Your Script:

"Earlier, things got heated.
Here is what I felt…
Here is what didn't work…
Here is what we need going forward."

Short. Clear. Clean.

Then you hand them their own mic:

"Tell me what you were feeling, and what you wish had happened instead."

You're not asking them to rewrite reality.
You're asking them to name it.

Naming builds honesty.
Blaming breaks safety.

We choose honesty.

Stage 3: Rebuild With Agreements, Not Just Apologies

Parents often treat repair like a scavenger hunt for the words "I'm sorry."

But apologies don't change patterns.
Agreements change patterns.

Apology = emotion

Agreement = action

You end the repair moment with one simple sentence:

"Next time, here's what we both agree to try."

Not a speech.
Not a list of twelve commandments.

One actionable shift—
easy to remember, hard to argue with.

Examples:

"We will both pause before raising our voices."

"We will use the safe word before we get overwhelmed."

"You will speak respectfully, and I will listen without interrupting."

"We will take a break when tone changes, then come back to finish."

Agreements create a roadmap.
Roadmaps reduce chaos.
Less chaos = more trust.

WHAT REPAIR LOOKS LIKE WITH LITTLE KIDS

Let's make this practical.

Your 7-year-old melts down because you said, "No snacks before dinner."

They:

yell

throw a toy

maybe slam a door

Most parents:

lecture

threaten

or give them the snack just to end the scene

Emotional repair looks like this instead:

Reset

"Let's pause. We'll talk when your body feels calm again."

Naming

"When I said no to the snack, you got very upset.
It's okay to feel mad.
It's not okay to throw things."

Agreement

"Next time you're mad, try sitting on the couch or taking deep breaths. I'll help you."

Simple. Predictable. Repeatable.

You're teaching emotional literacy and emotional safety at the same time.

WHAT REPAIR LOOKS LIKE WITH TEENS

Your teen snaps:

"Ugh, why are you always on my back?!"

The old script is:

"Watch your tone!"

"You don't talk to me like that!"

or you walk away hurt and silent.

Repair looks like:

Reset

"Let's take a minute. We'll talk after we cool down."

Naming

"When you spoke to me that way, it crossed a line.
I felt disrespected, and that doesn't work in this home."

Agreement

"Next time, if you're annoyed, say 'I need a moment.'
I'll give you space, and then we'll finish the conversation."

You're not trying to win.
You're trying to lead.

Teens may roll their eyes at the process...
but they blossom under that kind of leadership.

WHAT REPAIR LOOKS LIKE WITH ADULT CHILDREN

(The Gray-Haired Toddler Stage)

Yes... even grown kids need repair.
Sometimes especially grown kids.

Your adult child:

storms out

hangs up the phone

talks sideways

disrespects your time or your home

Repair looks like:

Reset

"We'll talk after we've both had time to settle."

Naming

"I love you, and I won't be spoken to that way.
That tone is not acceptable with me."

Agreement

"Next time, let's schedule the conversation instead of reacting in the moment."

You don't chase.
You don't beg.
You don't collapse.

You lead.

Repair with adult kids doesn't require you to apologize for their behavior.
It requires you to keep the boundary while you reopen the door.

THE BIG MYTH: "If I Repair, I'm Letting Them Off the Hook"

False.

Repair isn't removing consequences.
Repair is removing chaos.

You can keep every consequence and still repair with:

grace

clarity

structure

emotional sobriety

Your child should feel your love, not your leash.

Repair is not weakness.
Repair is wisdom.

THE SAINT REPAIR FRAMEWORK

(Put this on the Fridge)

One pause.
One truth.
One agreement.
One reset.

That's it.

Four steps.
Four beats.

A rhythm your home can follow even when emotions run high.

HOW REPAIR CHANGES A CHILD PERMANENTLY

Children who grow up in homes with structured repair learn:

Conflict is survivable.

Feelings can be expressed safely.

Boundaries don't break relationships.

Accountability isn't punishment.

Love isn't fragile.

Respect returns faster when everyone takes responsibility.

Children who grow up without repair learn:

Conflict is dangerous.

Emotions must be hidden.

Parents are unpredictable.

Disrespect becomes a communication style.

Apologies are weapons, not bridges.

Guilt replaces growth.

You are teaching your child the emotional culture of their future.

Repair is the cornerstone of that culture.

THE REPAIR CHECKLIST

(Use After Any Storm)

Ask yourself:

Am I calm enough to talk?

Can I name what happened without attacking?

Can I validate my child's feelings without excusing the behavior?

Can I ask them to share without interrogating them?

Can we end with one clear agreement?

Can we start fresh tomorrow without reopening the wound?

If you can check these boxes, you are parenting at a level many adults never experienced as children.

And that, Saint, is generational repair in real time.

MINI TRUTH BOMBS

A repaired home is stronger than a perfect one.
Accountability builds trust, not fear.
The real storm ends when calm walks back in.

REFLECT & RESET

What storms in my home still need repair—not erasing, but honest rebuilding?

Which step is hardest for me—pause, truth, agreement, or reset?

What will I practice this week to rebuild emotional safety in our home?

FINAL SAINT LINE

Repair is how love grows its backbone.

CHAPTER TWENTY-ONE

The last lesson

There comes a moment in every parent's life when everything slows down.
Not because the house is finally quiet—
but because *you* are.

It's the moment after every storm...
after the disrespect...
after the repairs...
after the consequences...
after the tears, the prayers, the boundaries, and the breakthroughs.

You sit still for the first time in months and whisper:

"I didn't raise a dependent.
I raised someone who can stand."

This is *The Last Lesson*.
And here's the truth:

The last lesson is not what your child learns.
The last lesson is what *you* learn.

THE REVEAL — THE MOMENT, YOU REALIZE YOU DID ENOUGH

It hits softly.
It hits suddenly.
It hits like a deep breath you didn't know you were holding.

You realize:

You didn't just keep them alive.
You didn't just fight the patterns.
You didn't just survive the seasons.

You prepared a human being.

A human who will one day:

- Stand up
- Fall down
- Rise again
- Love better
- Try harder
- Learn faster
- Respect deeper
- And eventually thank you

This is the graduation moment *you* receive.

THE SHIFT — FROM PARENT TO LEADER

Here's the quiet truth every parent eventually meets:

Parenting ends.
Leadership lasts.

One day, the tasks fall away:

- No more backpack checks
- No more tone reminders
- No more chore charts
- No more curfew battles
- No more emotional refereeing

But leadership?
Leadership becomes the voice inside their head.

Your calm tone becomes their emotional thermostat.
Your boundaries become their compass.
Your money policies become their financial survival.
Your consequences become their character.

The Last Lesson is this:

You cannot protect them forever.
But you can prepare them forever.

THE PRACTICAL CORE — WHAT ADULT CHILDREN ACTUALLY NEED

Adult children don't need rescuing.
They need modeling.

They don't need guilt.
They need guidance.

They don't need a soft landing.
They need a steady path.

The essentials:

1. Respect That Travels

Tone, punctuality, and accountability follow them everywhere.

2. Boundaries That Lead

"No" is not rejection.
"No" is direction.

3. Money Rules That Protect Peace

Cash App culture ends at your door.
Contribution is adulthood's first dialect.

4. Consequences That Teach, Not Terrify

You are building character, not compliance.

5. Repair That Restores Safety

Not Hallmark forgiveness.
Structured healing.

THE SAINT TRUTHS — YOUR FINAL HARD REALITY CHECK

TRUTH 1: Their choices reflect *them*, not you.
TRUTH 2: You can raise them right and still watch them struggle.
TRUTH 3: You are not responsible for who they refuse to become.
TRUTH 4: If you keep carrying them, they will forget they have legs.
TRUTH 5: Letting go is not losing them—letting go is releasing them into adulthood.

These are the truths that free the parent and mature the child.

THE TURN — WHEN YOU STEP BACK SO THEY CAN STEP UP

Here it is in one sentence:

A child becomes an adult the moment the parent stops shielding them from adulthood.

Not with coldness.
Not with distance.
With clarity.
With love.
With boundaries.

You look them in the eye and say:

"I am confident in your ability to figure it out for yourself."

That sentence becomes their armor.
Their anchor.
Their inner compass.

THE SPIRITUAL ANCHOR — GOD SAW ALL OF IT

Every tear you held back.
Every prayer whispered at midnight.
Every moment you showed restraint when your heart wanted to yell.
Every time you chose teaching over controlling.
Every quiet moment when you wondered,
"Am I doing this right?"

God saw:

- Your endurance
- Your tenderness
- Your calm spine
- Your courage
- Your leadership

Your strength didn't come from perfection—
it came from perseverance.

THE LAST LESSON CHECKLIST

Ask yourself:

✓ What am I still carrying that my child must learn to carry?
✓ Where am I rescuing instead of releasing?
✓ What boundary needs one final reinforcement?
✓ What habit of mine must shift for their growth?
✓ What legacy will this chapter leave in their memory?

Because this isn't the end—
this is the handoff.

MINI TRUTH BOMBS — CHAPTER TWENTY-ONE

The moment you stop rescuing is the moment they start rising.
Release is not abandonment—release is assignment.
Love prepares. Fear controls. Wisdom lets go.
Parenting ends. Legacy begins.
The last lesson shapes the future more than the first one ever did.

REFLECT & RESET

Where do I need to step back so my child can step forward?

What belief about parenting do I need to retire?

What legacy do I want this final chapter to leave?

Today's Tweak:
Choose one area where you will begin releasing responsibility to your child—
and let them rise into it.

FINAL SAINT LINE

Raise your child with love. Lead them with truth. And when the moment comes...let them rise.

CHAPTER TWENTY-TWO

How to make it stick for life

There comes a point in parenting when you look around your home, look at your child, look at your calendar, and whisper to yourself:

"Okay...but how do I make this LAST?"

Because anybody can parent for a week.
Anybody can hold a boundary for a moment.
Anybody can have one good day of tone resets and calm spines.

But raising a respectful human being?
Creating a home that stays steady?
Becoming the parent your future grandbabies will thank?

That requires more than momentum.
It requires *method*.

This final chapter is your blueprint for transformation that doesn't fade or flicker or fall apart when life gets loud.
This is how you turn a season of change… into a lifestyle of leadership.

Let's build the Saint Standard for life.

THE HOOK — Change Isn't a Moment. It's a Method.

You didn't walk through 21 chapters just to slide back into chaos.

You came here for peace that stays,
respect that returns,
and patterns that hold when your child is pushing every button you own.

Here's the truth no parenting book puts on the cover:

The secret to lasting change is not intensity — it's rhythm.

Small shifts.
Daily consistency.
Predictable leadership.
Repeat, repeat, repeat.

When your child realizes this is who you are now —
not a phase, not a mood, not a trial run —
they upgrade right along with you.

That's the magic.

THE FOUR PILLARS OF CHANGE THAT LASTS

These four pillars hold up every healthy home.
You strengthen these, and respect becomes natural instead of negotiated.

PILLAR 1 — CLARITY

Kids cannot follow what they cannot see.

Clarity means:
- short expectations
- simple standards
- rules written, said, and lived with consistency
- consequences that don't depend on your mood

Clarity is kindness in blueprint form.

TRUTH BOMB:
A child can't walk straight in a foggy house.

PILLAR 2 — CONSISTENCY

Clarity is the map.
Consistency is the gas.

Consistency is your superpower:
- same expectations on Monday and Saturday
- same tone when you're rested and when you're tired

- same consequence when they test you and when they charm you

Children don't need perfection.
They need *predictability*.

TRUTH BOMB:
If your boundary changes daily, your child won't change at all.

PILLAR 3 — CONNECTION

Respect cannot grow in a cold house.

Connection is:
- listening
- repairing after storms
- celebrating effort
- speaking kindly
- staying emotionally available without being emotionally drained

Connection is the warmth that makes boundaries feel safe, not scary.

TRUTH BOMB:
Kids follow leaders they feel connected to.

PILLAR 4 — CALIBRATION

Parenting isn't a straight line — it's a series of upgrades.

Calibration means:
- adjusting the rules as maturity grows
- increasing responsibility with age
- shifting tone, access, chores, and expectations as needed

Not because you're inconsistent —
but because growth requires evolution.

TRUTH BOMB:
Stagnant parenting creates stagnant kids.

THE SAINT METHOD: FIVE HABITS THAT MAKE IT STICK FOR LIFE

Do these consistently and your home will shift permanently.

Habit 1 — Start Over Every Morning

Yesterday is gone.
You don't drag old storms into new sunshine.

Script:
"New day. New tone. New chance."

Fresh starts build emotional safety.

Habit 2 — Speak in Systems, Not Speeches

Systems run your home when emotions don't.

Examples:
- Phone Dock Rule
- Try Again Doorway
- Weekly Respect Check-In
- Privilege Pause
- 24-Hour Reset

Your new mantra:
"If I system it, I don't have to stress it."

Habit 3 — Adopt the Zero-Chase Policy

No more chasing your child with:
- reminders
- emotions
- explanations
- apologies

You set the boundary.
You follow the policy.
You stay seated.

Nothing teaches respect faster.

Habit 4 — Make Repair a Ritual

Every storm ends the same way:

Pause → Truth → Agreement → Reset

Your child learns:
- conflict is survivable
- boundaries don't break relationships
- accountability isn't punishment
- emotional maturity is a skill

Repair is emotional wealth.

Habit 5 — Model the Calm You Expect

You are the thermostat —
your tone sets the temperature of the home.

Your calm spine becomes their blueprint for adulthood.

TRUTH BOMB:
Your child learns how to treat you by watching how you treat yourself.

THE LONG GAME — WHAT CHANGE ACTUALLY LOOKS LIKE

Month 1 — Resistance

They test you.
Side-eye you.
Perform dramatic monologues at 8 p.m.

Good.
The pattern is cracking.

Month 2 — Adjustment

They begin:
- pausing
- resetting tone
- accepting consequences quicker
- contributing more

Your home exhales.

Month 3 — Respect Returns

It hits suddenly:
- calmer mornings
- fewer arguments
- smoother routines
- clearer expectations
- better conversations

And you realize:

You didn't just change your child.
You changed the emotional culture of your home.

THE REAL SECRET — YOU MADE IT STICK BECAUSE YOU STUCK WITH YOU

This wasn't about perfection.
This was about predictability.
You stopped reacting.
You started leading.

Calm with a backbone.
Firm with a soft voice.
Strong without being loud.

You became the parent your child grows into —
not the one they outgrow.

REFLECT & RESET — THE LIFETIME VERSION

Which pillar (clarity, consistency, connection, calibration) needs strengthening in my home?

What daily habit will anchor my leadership when emotions run high?

What legacy of respect do I want my child to remember 10, 20, 40 years from now?

Today's Tweak:

Choose ONE habit and practice it for 30 days.

Just one.

Watch your home shift.

FINAL SAINT LINE

Respect that begins today can last a lifetime — when you lead like it already belongs to you.

APPENDIX A

THE CALM SPINE SELF-ASSESSMENT™
(How Much Backbone Do You REALLY Have?)

Before you flip the page and congratulate yourself for surviving this book, let's take a moment of holy honesty.

Every parent *thinks* they have a Calm Spine...
until the dishwasher door slams...
or the teen sighs like their lungs are filing for bankruptcy...
or an adult child texts, *"Did you send it yet?"*
and suddenly your spine folds like a Dollar Tree lawn chair.

This assessment is your mirror — funny, real, and surprisingly accurate.
Grade yourself.
Laugh at yourself.
And then use these results to decide what to work on next.

Grab a pen.
A snack.
And let's see what your spine is giving today.

HOW TO TAKE THE QUIZ

Read each question.
Circle A, B, C, or D.

Keep your score.

No cheating — that already tells me your spine is in danger.

Each A = 4 points

Each B = 3 points

Each C = 2 points

Each D = 1 point

SECTION 1 — TONE & EMOTIONAL STABILITY

1. When your child raises their voice, your first instinct is:

A. Pause and breathe like a Buddhist monk.

B. Count to three and choose peace... mostly.

C. Match their volume like it's karaoke night.

D. Immediately forget the English language.

2. When your child slams a door, you:

A. Say calmly, "Try again with respect."

B. Raise an eyebrow but let it slide.

C. Slam another door back (for symmetry).

D. Consider moving to another state.

3. When conflict hits, your tone is:

A. Smooth, steady, unshakeable.

B. Calm-ish with occasional spice.

C. Loud enough to activate neighborhood dogs.

D. Emotional free-fall.

SECTION 2 — BOUNDARIES & CONSEQUENCES

4. How many times do you repeat a rule?
A. Once. The boundary is the boundary.
B. Twice, because you're human.
C. Fourteen times and a TED Talk.
D. You stopped counting in 2018.

5. When disrespect happens, you:
A. Pause the privilege — calmly.
B. Correct the behavior with mild heat.
C. Argue for 45 minutes.
D. Cry in the bathroom and hope for peace.

6. When consequences are required, you:
A. Follow through instantly.
B. Follow through eventually.
C. Threaten more than you enforce.
D. Let Jesus take the wheel.

SECTION 3 — SYSTEMS & CONSISTENCY

7. Your home runs on:
A. Policies and predictable routines.
B. Mostly consistent structure.
C. Vibes and whatever feels right.
D. Controlled chaos and Google Calendar confusion.

8. If someone asked your child what the rules are, they would say:

A. "Easy. We all know them."

B. "Most of them, yeah."

C. "It depends on Mom's mood."

D. "Rules? Never met her."

9. When you set a consequence, how long does it last?

A. The full duration, no exceptions.

B. Until someone cries... including you.

C. 3–7 minutes, depending on phone storage.

D. What consequence?

SECTION 4 — COMMUNICATION & SCRIPTS

10. Your parenting sentences average:

A. 7–10 words (Saint Approved).

B. A respectable paragraph.

C. Emotional monologue.

D. A three-part Netflix documentary.

11. When your child uses the wrong tone, you:

A. Say, "Try again with respect."

B. Give a verbal side-eye.

C. Start lecturing like you're running for office.

D. Ask yourself how early bedtime laws can become federal legislation.

12. If your teen texts you "Wyd," you respond:

A. "Waiting for respect."

B. "Try again."

C. "WHO ARE YOU TALKING TO?"

D. Leave them on read — you've evolved past this.

SECTION 5 — EMOTIONAL RESCUE & GUILT

13. When your child makes a mistake, you:

A. Guide, not rescue.

B. Help... but wish you didn't.

C. Fix everything before they even ask.

D. Become DoorDash for their emotions.

14. When guilt hits, you:

A. Acknowledge it but don't let it lead.

B. Battle it with mixed success.

C. Follow guilt like GPS.

D. Make decisions exclusively from emotional panic.

15. When your child cries, you:

A. Stay calm and stick to the boundary.

B. Offer comfort AND accountability.

C. Fold like fresh laundry.

D. Immediately question every choice you've ever made.

SECTION 6 — RESPECT & HOUSE CULTURE

16. Your home's respect level is:

A. Stable and consistent.

B. Improving with daily effort.

C. Hit-or-miss depending on astrology.

D. Currently sponsored by chaos.

17. When disrespect shows up, you:

A. Address it immediately and calmly.

B. Wait until the right moment.

C. Wait until the NEXT moment.

D. Wait until you explode.

18. Your kids would describe you as:

A. Calm but firm.

B. Fair but emotional.

C. "Sometimes chill, sometimes volcano."

D. "I don't know, ask the therapist."

SECTION 7 — THE SAINT SPINE SIGNATURE QUESTIONS

19. Do you use a Safe Word Protocol?

A. Yes, consistently.

B. Sometimes.

C. We tried once.

D. Safe word??

20. When the world pushes back on your child, you:

A. Let natural consequences teach.

B. Guide from the sidelines.

C. Rescue because "they're not ready."

D. Email the teacher, manager, and housing office.

21. When it's time to reset the home, you:

A. Host a family meeting like a CEO.

B. Attempt a reset with moderate success.

C. Try but get derailed by snacks, phones, or tears.

D. Reset? The home reset *you*.

SCORING

Add your points.

40–50 POINTS → THE SAINT SPINE (Elite Tier)

You are the blueprint.
Your boundaries travel.
Your tone is steady.
Your house runs on clarity.
You are raising adults, not dependents.
Book 2 will only make you stronger.

30–39 POINTS → THE EMERGING SPINE (Growing Tier)

You've got structure, humor, and momentum.
A few leaks — nothing a boundary tune-up can't fix.
Your Calm Spine is loading... 78%.

20–29 POINTS → THE FLEXIBLE SPINE (Wobble Tier)

You are doing your best with what you have.
But the kids definitely know your weak spots.
No shame — just systems needed.
Book 2 is about to change your whole house.

0–19 POINTS → NO SPINE (The Gray-Haired Toddler Has You in a Chokehold)

Saint...
You are parenting from vibes, exhaustion, and leftover prayers.
But you made it to this book, so your comeback starts TODAY.
Don't spiral — just systemize.
Your new spine is under construction.

FINAL SAINT LINE FOR APPENDIX A

A Calm Spine isn't something you're born with — it's something you build.
And today, you started building.

APPENDIX B

Which Parent Are You?

A Humor Quiz for Saint Parents Who Need the Truth Gently (But Quickly)

Because sometimes the best way to grow... is to laugh at yourself first.

Welcome to the only parenting quiz that tells the truth without dragging you.
Each question has four options — choose the one that *most consistently* matches your vibe.

Grab a pen. Grab your honesty. Grab your water because the truth tends to be a little dehydrating.

1. When your child raises their tone, you...

A. Match it like it's karaoke night.
B. Calmly say, "Pause. Try again."
C. Walk away before you end up on the news.
D. Explain for 12 minutes why tone matters, then apologize for over-explaining.

2. When your teen says, "I'll do it later," you...

A. Believe them. Again.
B. Set a timer and point to the chore list like a CEO.
C. Do it yourself because it's easier than fighting.
D. Deliver a motivational speech that ends with, "Back in my day..."

3. When a consequence is needed, you...

A. Announce a punishment so dramatic you could never keep it.
B. Deliver one sentence: "Privilege paused until respect returns."
C. Fold like a beach chair.
D. Negotiate like you're at a yard sale.

4. When your child blames you for something wild, like rain or algebra, you...

A. Defend yourself like you're on trial.
B. Say, "I hear you're upset — what's your plan?"
C. Cry in the bathroom (or the car).
D. Pull out childhood photos to prove you were a good parent.

5. When disrespect enters the room, you...

A. Come in hot.

B. Pause, breathe, and calmly reset the tone.

C. Pretend you didn't hear it.

D. Ask, "Do we need a family meeting... again?"

6. Your discipline style is closest to...

A. Grand finale fireworks. Every consequence is BIG.

B. Quiet, steady, predictable — you've got a calm spine.

C. "I don't have a style. I have exhaustion."

D. Google-in-the-moment parenting.

7. Your communication motto is...

A. "You got one more time."

B. "One sentence. One boundary. One consequence."

C. "Lord, give me strength."

D. "Let me explain what I meant... and also what I didn't mean."

8. When your child asks for money, you...

A. Already reaching for your purse before they finish the sentence.

B. Ask for a plan, proof, and timeline.

C. Cash App first, consequences later.
D. Start explaining interest rates from 1983.

9. When conflict happens, you...

A. Dive in immediately — emotions first, logic later.
B. Pause, reset, revisit when everyone's calm.
C. Sweep it under the rug with the other 47 unresolved conversations.
D. Hold a TED Talk.

10. When you think about parenting, you feel...

A. Tired in the bones.
B. Confident, structured, and peaceful (most days).
C. Like you're raising a tiny lawyer.
D. On the brink of Googling "boarding school."

Now, Count Your Letters

Mostly A's — The Crisis Coordinator

You parent with passion, volume, and quick reflexes.
Your heart is huge, but your reactions are faster than your strategy.

Your growth edge: slow down the storm inside yourself so your child can't surf it.

Tip: Adopt the Calm Spine Script — "We'll talk when we're calm."

Mostly B's — The Calm CEO (Saint Level)

You run your home like a serene Fortune 500 company. Predictable consequences. Clear boundaries. A voice smoother than a gospel solo.
Your kids may not *like* it, but they respect it.

Your growth edge: Keep going. Don't let guilt talk you out of your greatness.

Mostly C's — The Soft-Spine Saint

You're loving, gentle, and empathetic — but your boundaries are made of warm noodles.
Kids adore you.
But they also run circles around you.

Your growth edge: Move from comfort to clarity.
One sentence consequences. No back-and-forth.

Mostly D's — The Over-Explainer

You could host a parenting podcast today — you've got wisdom for days.
But your delivery is *long*, emotional, and exhausting (for you and for them).

Your growth edge: Shorten the sermon.
Long explanations dilute strong boundaries.

Your Bonus "Saint Score"

Just for fun — circle your vibe:

Crisp Spine — My boundaries are clear.
Warm Spine — I'm consistent, but feelings get me sometimes.
Soft Spine — I need courage and consequences.
No Spine — Lord, rebuild me.

You now know exactly which muscles to strengthen in Book 2.

Closing Line for the Appendix B

Awareness is the first fence. When you know your patterns, you can finally change them.

APPENDIX C

THE SAINT PARENTING TOOLKIT
(Respect Reset • Calm Spine Scripts • House Rules Blueprint)

This appendix is your *practical afterburner*.

The book taught the mindset.

Your home taught the patterns.

This appendix teaches the implementation — quickly, calmly, and without theatrics.

Everything here is designed to:

Save your voice

Strengthen your leadership

Reduce daily disrespect

Build respect that travels

And help your home function like a well-run organization instead of a group project gone wrong

Let's build your Saint system.

SECTION 1 — The 7-Day Respect Reset Plan

(A simple reboot for chaotic households)

This mini-bootcamp is your "reset button."

Follow it exactly as written — no speeches, no extras, no new rules mid-week.

DAY 1 — The Announcement

Script:
"Family, we're doing a 7-Day Respect Reset. It's simple, calm, and consistent. Everyone participates — including me."

Action:

Restate 3–5 house standards.

Choose one consequence for the week (privilege pause, phone dock, early curfew).

Tone:
Warm. Clear. Bored of chaos.

DAY 2 — Tone & Clarity

Today's focus: Correct tone in real time.

Family script:
"Try again with respect."

Parent rule:

No lectures.

No attitude.

Just calm redirection.

DAY 3 — Responsibilities First

Focus: Chores and tasks before leisure.

Script:
"When responsibility is done, access returns."

Action:

No TV, Wi-Fi, or outings until tasks are complete.

DAY 4 — The Communication Reset

Everyone practices:

Speaking clearly

Speaking directly

Speaking without mumbling or rolling eyes

Script:
"Say that again with clarity."

Kids HATE this day.
Parents LOVE this day.

DAY 5 — Accountability Check-In

5-minute meeting:

What worked?

What didn't?

What needs a reset for tomorrow?

Script:
"I'm proud of the progress. Here's one thing we'll tighten."

DAY 6 — Privilege & Consequence Consistency

Today is for enforcing consequences calmly, no matter how you feel.

Script:
"The consequence is automatic. We'll try again tomorrow."

Goal:
Teach predictability > punishment.

DAY 7 — The Celebration & Agreement

Close with gratitude:
"I saw real effort this week."

Then get ONE agreement for the next 30 days, such as:

"We'll all manage tone."

"Responsibilities before Wi-Fi."

"We pause conversations when disrespect shows up."

This ends the week on hope, not heaviness.

SECTION 2 — The Calm Spine Script Library

(Your cheat sheet for any parenting situation)

Short. Clean. PG-friendly.
These scripts are your new Saint Soundtrack.

TONE & RESPECT SCRIPTS

"Try again with respect."

"Pause. Reset your tone."

"We'll talk when our voices match."

"Start over with calm."

DISRESPECT/ATTITUDE SCRIPTS

"I don't receive that tone. Try again."

"This conversation pauses until we're calm."

"Respect first — then access."

CONSEQUENCE SCRIPTS

"The consequence is automatic."

"Phone is paused until respect returns."

"Curfew resets this weekend. Try again next week."

"Chores first. Privileges after."

GRAY-HAIRED TODDLER STAGE SCRIPTS (ADULT KIDS)

"I love you, and I won't be spoken to that way."

"We can discuss this when we both have clarity."

"Let's schedule this conversation instead of reacting in the moment."

MONEY BOUNDARY SCRIPTS

"I only loan money once a year."

"No cash — yes plan."

"I support effort, not emergencies you could have prevented."

SAFE WORD PROTOCOL SCRIPTS

"Safe word: pause and return in 20 minutes."

"We pause the conversation, not the consequence."

REPAIR AFTER THE STORM SCRIPTS

"Here's what I felt and here's what I need moving forward."

"Tell me what you were feeling and what you wish had happened instead."

"Next time, here's what we both agree to try."

EXIT LINE FOR ANY CRISIS

"I'm confident in your ability to figure it out for yourself."

Every Saint parent needs this.

SECTION 3 — The House Rules Blueprint

(A customizable template for peace, clarity, and respect)

Print this.
Post it.
Refer to it.
Live by it.

This is your official Angela Saint Home Policy — PG tone, calm spine, zero chaos.

1. HOUSE STANDARDS

Choose 3–5. Examples:

Speak respectfully.

Responsibilities before leisure.

Keep common areas clean.

Honor bedtime and morning routines.

Conversations pause when tone drops.

TRUTH BOMB:
 Peace needs structure. Chaos grows where rules hide.

2. TECH & PHONE POLICY

Phones dock by ___ PM.

No tech until responsibilities are done.

Parental access during safety checks.

Wi-Fi pauses for disrespect, missing responsibilities, or unsafe behavior.

Script:
"Technology is a privilege, not a right."

3. CHORE SYSTEM

Assign:

Daily

Weekly

Monthly

Include consequences:

Missed chore = chore + bonus task.

4. CURFEW & SCHEDULE STRUCTURE

Curfew is _____.
Violation resets curfew for ____ days.
Family calendar reviewed weekly.

5. RESPECT POLICY

Tone matters.

Volume matters.

Word choice matters.

Disrespect = automatic consequence.

Conversations pause when triggered.

6. PRIVILEGE PAUSE FRAMEWORK

Used for:

Tone issues

Responsibility issues

Repeated disrespect

Lasts: 24 hours (or as defined).
Restored through:

Calm tone

Completed responsibilities

Re-engagement in good faith

7. CONSEQUENCE MENU

Choose 3 to use consistently:

Phone pause (24 hours)

Early curfew

Chore swap

Quiet hour

No rides for 48 hours

Limited tech access

Script:
"The consequence is automatic — not emotional."

8. FAMILY CHECK-IN ROUTINE

Weekly 10-minute meeting:

One win

One problem

One adjustment

Keeps resentment low and respect high.

FINAL SAINT LINE FOR APPENDIX C

A calm spine isn't a personality.
It's a policy.
Build it, live it, and watch your home transform.

APPENDIX D

THE CALM SPINE SELF-ASSESSMENT
(A Funny But Deadly Accurate Checkup for Parents)

If you've made it this far in the book, give yourself a praise dance.

Now comes the fun part — grading yourself.

No shame.

No guilt.

Just an honest, hilarious, reality-check moment between you, your parenting, and the calm spine you're building.

Grab a pen.

Or just shout the answers out loud like you're on a game show.

Either way, let's see where your leadership stands.

SECTION 1 — THE CALM SPINE QUIZ

(Circle all that apply. Be honest — the walls can't hear you.)

1. When disrespect shows up, I usually...

A. Address it calmly with a clean script.
B. Match their tone like I'm auditioning for a telenovela.
C. Pretend I didn't hear it because I'm tired and Jesus knows my heart.

2. When consequences are needed...

A. I apply them immediately and consistently.
B. I threaten consequences and hope they behave out of fear.
C. I forget the consequence before the child does.

3. When my child blames me for something ridiculous...

A. I stay in leadership and redirect responsibility.
B. I over-explain my entire life story.
C. I start thinking maybe *I* caused the global pandemic.

4. Tone correction in my home looks like...

A. "Try again with respect."
B. "WHO ARE YOU TALKING TO?"
C. Me staring at the ceiling like I'm waiting for a sign.

5. When I'm triggered...

A. I pause and reset the conversation.
B. I say something I regret and then need my own repair moment.
C. I fake calm while actually plotting an escape to Target.

6. Natural consequences...

A. I use them. They work.
B. I forget them and just yell louder.
C. What are those again?

7. My follow-through with rules is...

A. Strong and steady.
B. Depends on how my day went.
C. Somewhere between "household CEO" and "please stop talking to me."

8. My child's tone changes and I...

A. Pause the conversation.
B. Clap back.
C. Pretend I didn't hear it because I'm not ready.

9. After conflict, I...

A. Repair with structure (pause, truth, agreement, reset).
B. Hug it out even though nothing was fixed.
C. Move on but mentally resent everyone in the house.

10. In general, my parenting spine is...

A. Steel.
B. Aluminum foil.
C. Noodle.

SECTION 2 — SCORING

Count your A's, B's, and C's.

MOSTLY A's — "THE SAINT LEADER"

You're giving calm, clear, consistent leadership.
Your child sees you as a safe, steady presence.
Your spine = titanium.
Your house = order with love.
Your future = stress declining like gas prices in your dreams.

Keep going.
And teach a friend.

MOSTLY B's — "THE WOBBLE SPINE"

You know what to do...
but emotional turbulence keeps pulling you off course.

Your homework:

shorten your scripts

tighten your follow-through

stop giving speeches longer than the State of the Union

You're close.
One week of consistency will change everything.

MOSTLY C's — "THE GRAY-HAIRED TODDLER PARENTING STYLE"

No judgment.
It's giving survival mode.
It's giving "baby, I'm tired."
But guess what?

You showed up.
You're reading this.
And you're about to pivot.

Your next step:
Pick ONE area — tone, chores, consequences, or boundaries.
Start there.
Small shifts change big patterns.

Your spine is not broken.
It's just sleepy.

SECTION 3 — YOUR PERSONAL CALM SPINE PLAN

Fill this out and tape it somewhere you'll see it daily.

My biggest challenge area:

One script I will use this week:

One consequence I will apply consistently:

My new agreement with myself:

How I will model calm leadership:

This is your growth blueprint.
The family follows the parent — and you're leading them toward clarity, peace, and respect.

FINAL SAINT LINE FOR APPENDIX D

A calm spine isn't something you're born with. It's something you build — one choice, one boundary, one deep breath at a time.

APPENDIX E

THE PARENTING RED FLAGS CHECKLIST
(A Hilarious Reality Check for Every Household)

Every family has patterns, quirks, chaos pockets, and "don't start with me today" triggers.
Most people ignore them…
until the house feels like a group project where only one person is doing the work.

So let's name the red flags with humor —
because when you can laugh about it,
you can lead through it.

Check every red flag that applies to you *or* your child.
No shame — only elevation.

SECTION 1 — RED FLAGS FOR PARENTS

(If you see 3 or more, congratulations — you're normal.)

**1. You remind your child to do something…

then do it yourself because it's faster.

2. You threaten consequences you know you don't have the energy to enforce.

3. You yell, "STOP YELLING!" and only realize the irony later.

4. You keep buying snacks for a child who treats you like their unpaid personal shopper.

5. You give 45-minute lectures no one asked for... including you.

6. You apologize to strangers but argue with your own child about tone.

7. You pray before entering their room because you don't know what ecosystem is growing in there.

8. You say, "This is the LAST TIME!" at least twice a week.

9. You've confiscated a phone and then forgot where you hid it.

10. You've whispered, "Lord, give me strength or give me Wi-Fi," at least once.

TRUTH BOMB:
Awareness is the first boundary.

SECTION 2 — RED FLAGS FOR KIDS (ALL AGES)

(Circle every one that makes you sigh.)

1. They say "I'm grown" but can't keep track of their own charger.

2. They act shocked when consequences arrive... even though they RSVP'd with their behavior.

3. They roll their eyes so hard you're worried they'll see the ancestors.

4. They mumble entire conversations like they're being paid per syllable withheld.

5. They ask for rides but treat your car like a community trash can.

6. They wait until *you* start cooking to suddenly say they're starving.

7. They lose things daily but somehow never lose their attitude.

8. They say "I forgot" like it's a medical diagnosis.

9. They treat chores like punishment but treat TikTok like a full-time job.

10. They believe the universe revolves around their mood swings.

TRUTH BOMB:
Chaos is a habit — but so is respect.

SECTION 3 — RED FLAGS FOR THE HOUSEHOLD ENERGY

(This reveals the system, not just the people.)

1. Everyone is tired, but nobody is resting.

2. You haven't had a peaceful dinner since Obama's first term.

3. Doors slam more than they open.

4. Tone resets are rare, but tension is common.

5. Conversations turn into arguments faster than microwaved popcorn.

6. People avoid each other to avoid conflict.

7. The family calendar is chaos with color coding.

8. Accountability only shows up when someone is in trouble.

9. Respect is mentioned but not practiced.

10. Everyone walks on eggshells — including the dog.

TRUTH BOMB:
A household is only as peaceful as its patterns.

SECTION 4 — YOUR RED FLAG REPORT CARD

Count the number you selected in each section.

0–3 flags:

"Calm-ish Kingdom"
There's structure.
There's peace.
There's clarity.
You're thriving — with occasional chaos seasoning.

4–7 flags:

"Wobbly but Recoverable"
Your home is one reset meeting away from greatness.
Tighten the boundaries.
Shorten the speeches.
Choose consistency over drama.

8–12 flags:

"The Gray-Haired Toddler Energy Is Strong"
You are carrying too much, managing too much, and rescuing too much.
Your upgrade begins with ONE boundary this week.

13+ flags:

"Saint, Call the Meeting."
It's time for a household reboot.
The Annual Reset Meeting (Chapter 18) is your medicine.
Healing starts with one calm spine step.

SECTION 5 — THE RED FLAG REMEDY PLAN

Fill this out with honesty and a little humor:

The biggest red flag in my parenting:

The biggest red flag in my child's behavior:

One household red flag we must address:

What I'm proud of in our home:

What we will adjust starting today:

FINAL SAINT LINE FOR APPENDIX E

Red flags aren't failures — they're invitations.
And your family is ready for the upgrade.

APPENDIX F

THE CALM SPINE TOOLKIT

(The 10 Tools Every Parent Needs When Life Gets Loud)

This is your pocket guide.
Your emergency kit.
Your "Lord, give me strength or give me silence" survival pack.

Everything here is designed to take parents from chaos → clarity in ten seconds or less.

Let's go.

THE CALM SPINE TOOLKIT

(Choose your weapon wisely — some days you'll need all ten.)

TOOL 1 — The 10-Second Reset

When the tone shifts and your spirit says, *"Not today, Satan,"* use this.

How it works:
- One slow breath in
- One slow breath out

Then say:

"We'll talk when the tone returns."

It resets you *and* reroutes them.

TRUTH BOMB:

Calm is contagious — so is chaos. Choose the one you want spreading.

TOOL 2 — The One-Sentence Policy

Stop giving TED Talks.
Stop debating children with full Wi-Fi access.

Your new rule: Never exceed ten words.

Examples:
- "Phones dock at nine. Non-negotiable."
- "Respect first, conversation second."
- "Try again with a better tone."
- "Privilege paused. Reset tomorrow."

Short sentences carry big authority.

TOOL 3 — The Try Again Doorway

Every doorway becomes a reset point.

Kid tries you?
Rolls eyes?
Mumbles? Slams?

Say:
"Pause. Try again from the doorway."

They walk out... walk back in... and start over respectfully.

It's magical. Humbling. Unforgettable.

TOOL 4 — The Silent Treatment Shield

If they weaponize silence, flip it.

Script:
"We can talk when you're ready for respect."

Not emotional.
Not dramatic.
Just availability with boundaries.

They'll return calmer — and cuter.

TOOL 5 — The 7 p.m. Peace Rule

Saint Standard:
After 7 p.m., no heavy conversations, no arguments, no drama deep dives.

Evening hours distort emotions.

Script:
"This is not a 7 p.m. problem. We'll revisit tomorrow."

Protect your peace — and your sleep.

TOOL 6 — The Parent Time-Out (Yes, Really)

Kids aren't the only ones who need a breather.

Script:
"I need a minute so I lead with wisdom, not emotion."

Step away.
Drink water.
Reset like a CEO with a calling.

Come back with strategy, not smoke.

TOOL 7 — The Mirror Check

Before correcting your child, check *your* tone, posture, and presence.

Ask:

"Would I follow me right now?"

If not?
Reset before you lead.

This is the difference between dictatorship and leadership.

TOOL 8 — The Two-Question Rule

Your antidote to whining, chaos, and blame.

Ask:

What have you tried?

What's your plan?

It shifts responsibility from your spine... back onto theirs.

TOOL 9 — The Privilege Pause

Not punishment — pause.

Phones? Paused.
Wi-Fi? Paused.
Rides? Paused.
Friend time? Paused.
CashApp? Baby... paused.

Script:
"Privileges return when respect returns."

Clean. Clear. Calm. Effective.

TOOL 10 — The 24-Hour Refresh Rule

No grudges.
No reliving yesterday.

House rule:
"After 24 hours, we reset — not relive."

Conflict isn't a cage.
It's a classroom.

BONUS — THE EMERGENCY PRAYER

Use this when your last nerve starts packing a suitcase:

"Lord, help me lead with wisdom, love, and a calm spine.
Block my mouth when it needs blocking,
Strengthen my tone when it needs strength,
And remind me I'm raising someone's future coworker, spouse, neighbor, and leader.
Amen."

MINI TRUTH BOMBS — APPENDIX F

A calm spine teaches louder than a raised voice.
Boundaries work best when your tone works first.
Leadership is who you are when the house gets loud.
Your child is learning how to treat the world by how they treat you.

FINAL SAINT LINE FOR APPENDIX F

When you lead with a calm spine, your home learns to breathe again.

CONCLUSION

The New Respect Era Begins With You

Every family has a turning point — a moment when someone finally stands up, takes a breath, and says, *"This cycle ends with me."*

Saint, that someone is you.

You didn't just read a book.
You rebuilt the foundation of your home one truth, one boundary, one pause, one prayer at a time.

You shifted from panic to purpose.
From over-explaining to clear expectations.

From bulldozed to balanced.
From tired to trusted.

You learned that respect is not a demand — it's a culture.
A language.
A rhythm that returns when the adults in the home stop performing emotional CPR on everyone else and start leading with clarity.

And through these chapters, you've done exactly that.

You have rewritten the emotional blueprint of your family.

THE WORK YOU'VE DONE — AND WHY IT MATTERS

You learned the early signs:
the whining, the power grabs, the "gray-haired toddler" behaviors that sneak into your child's tone long before adulthood.

You learned the scripts:
the ten-word sentences that slice through chaos like a clean line of truth.

You learned the systems:

Safe Word Protocol

Unified Front Protocol

Responsibility Reset

Respect Restoration Plan

Emotional Sobriety

Annual Loan Rule

Office Hours

Money Firewall

You learned how predictable boundaries create predictable peace.

And you learned the most important truth of all:

You cannot teach what you won't model.
And you cannot model what you won't practice.

But you *did* practice.
You *did* shift.
You *did* show up — even in the messy parts.

Your home didn't need a new child.
It needed a new leader.

And now you are leading with the quiet authority of a parent who knows:

calm is power

clarity is kindness

consistency is respect

boundaries are love with a spine

Your children will remember this version of you.
Not the tired you.
Not the frustrated you.
Not the over-functioning, over-giving, over-explaining you.

They will remember the parent who finally said:

"No more chaos culture.
No more emotional storms.
This home will have peace."

And you meant it.

THE SHIFT THAT CHANGES EVERYTHING

When you lead differently, your children grow differently.
They rise to meet the strength in you.
They soften when your tone softens.
They stabilize when your boundaries stabilize.
They respect what you respect — starting with yourself.

This is the essence of parenting:
Not perfection.
Not endless giving.
Not rescuing or performing or exhausting yourself on the altar of trying.

Parenting is leadership.
And leadership is legacy.

You are building a legacy of:

clarity

accountability

emotional steadiness

boundaries that don't break

love that doesn't collapse

respect that travels

This is the kind of leadership that raises adults who know how to speak clearly, work responsibly, love respectfully, and move through the world with confidence.
This is the kind of leadership that ends generational foolishness.
This is the kind of leadership that changes the emotional climate of a household forever.

And you did that.
Chapter by chapter.
Shift by shift.

THE NEW ERA STARTS NOW

When you close this final page, your work is not over.
But it's no longer heavy.
It's no longer confusing.
It's no longer a guessing game.

You have a map now.
A framework.
A toolbox.
A calm spine.
A stronger voice.
A reset button.
A plan for the storms.
A blueprint for repair.
A house policy that can outlive any tantrum, any teen attitude, any adult child meltdown.

Respect is not a request anymore.
It's the new expectation.
The new atmosphere.
The new family standard.

And it begins with how you show up tomorrow morning.

Not perfect.
Not pressured.
Just present.
Prepared.
Clear.
Steady.

Consistent.
Loved and loving.

This is the new rhythm of your home.

WHERE YOU GO NEXT

This is the end of Book 1 —
but it is not the end of your transformation.

Book 2 is your next chapter:
Boundaries Without Bitterness.
Where you learn to hold your line without losing your joy, your softness, or your sanity.
Where money, time, energy, and emotional labor all get a fresh set of rules.
Where guilt no longer runs your home, and clarity becomes your new compass.

But for now?
Pause.
Take a breath.
Feel what you've done.

You didn't just read.
You rebuilt.

You didn't just learn.
You led.

You didn't just survive.
You reclaimed your crown.

FINAL TRUTH BOMB:

Respect grows where clarity lives. Peace follows where boundaries stand. And healing begins when you do.

FINAL SAINT LINE

Lead your home with a calm spine — and watch your legacy rise.

APPENDIX G

THE CALM SPINE SCORECARD
(Grade Your Growth — One Truth Bomb at a Time)

Welcome to the part of the book where you stop, smile, and get a little convicted.

This scorecard isn't about shame — it's about clarity.

It shows you where your spine is strong, where your tone is slipping, and where your boundaries could use a gym membership.

Answer each question with your first instinct.

No overthinking.

No essays.

No "well, sometimes, but only when Mercury is in retrograde."

Just honesty.

Circle: **A, B, or C**

A = Calm Spine Energy

B = Wobbly Spine, but trying

C = No Spine, baby — but that's why we're here

1. When your child raises their voice...

A — I pause and calmly say, "We'll talk when the tone returns."
B — I try to stay calm but sometimes match their volume.
C — Suddenly I'm auditioning for a reality show.

2. When you say NO...

A — You mean it. Period.
B — You mean it... until the whining hits maximum volume.
C — Your "no" is just a placeholder for a future "fine."

3. When your child blames you for their choices...

A — I shift to leadership: "What part is yours today?"
B — I explain myself into exhaustion.
C — I start doubting myself instantly.

4. When disrespect shows up...

A — Tone stops the conversation, not my emotions.
B — I correct it, but with a little heat.
C — I ignore it because I'm too tired for another showdown.

5. When chaos pops off at 8:59 p.m....

A — "This is not a nighttime problem. We'll revisit tomorrow."
B — Depends on the day and the snack I just ate.
C — I jump right in and regret it immediately.

6. When your grown child asks for money... again...

A — "This is your annual loan. What's your plan?"
B — *sighs* "How much is it this time?"
C — Sends it before they even finish typing.

7. When you're upset...

A — I take a parent time-out and return with clarity.
B — I try... but I talk before I'm ready.
C — I react first and breathe later.

8. When your child breaks a rule...

A — Consequence. Calm. Consistent.
B — Consequence... but with commentary.
C — Consequence depends on my mood, the weather, and the bills.

9. When a disagreement gets loud...

A — Safe word. Pause. Reset.
B — I try to slow it down.
C — The neighbors know our business.

10. When it's time to start fresh...

A — I use the 24-Hour Refresh Rule.
B — I forgive... eventually.
C — I carry yesterday into next week.

YOUR CALM SPINE SCORE

Count how many A's, B's, and C's you circled.

Mostly A's — SAINT STATUS

Your backbone is titanium with a velvet coating.
Your home may not be perfect, but your leadership is solid.
Keep going — you're modeling emotional maturity your child will carry into adulthood.

Mostly B's — SPINE UNDER CONSTRUCTION

You're growing.
You're learning.

You're building consistency.
This book was designed for YOU — keep applying the tools, and your home will shift faster than you expect.

Mostly C's — IT'S OKAY, BABY. HELP HAS ARRIVED.

You're not lost — you're overwhelmed.
You're not weak — you're tired.
These tools will change your life if you use them consistently.
Start with one tool per week and watch your confidence rise.

MINI TRUTH BOMBS FOR APPENDIX G

Growth starts with honesty, not perfection.
A calm spine is built, not born.
You can't teach what you won't practice.
Your child learns emotional leadership by watching yours.

ACKNOWLEDGMENTS

To every parent who ever cried in their car, prayed in their kitchen, or whispered "Lord, help me" under their breath — this book is for you.
Your courage, your consistency, and your commitment to raising respectful, responsible humans is sacred work.

To the mothers who feel unseen, the fathers who feel unheard, and the caregivers doing the job of three people with one paycheck — may this book remind you that your leadership matters, your boundaries matter, and YOU matter.

To my own family — thank you for teaching me the art, the humor, and the heart of parenting. Every lesson, every season, every curveball shaped this work.

And to every reader who turned these pages with hope in their hands:
Thank you for trusting me to sit at your kitchen table and speak life into your home.
You are the reason this book exists.

With gratitude and a calm spine,
Angela Saint

ABOUT THE AUTHOR

Angela Saint is a wife, mother, and educator who turned decades of exhaustion, trial-and-error parenting, and relentless love into a movement. With a Master's in Education, a Bachelor's in Psychology, and thirty years of real-world parenting receipts, she speaks straight to the heart of parents who are tired of being bulldozed in their own homes.

Angela doesn't sugarcoat the truth — she serves it with a calm spine, humor, and hope. Her Parenting/Adulting series blends real-life stories, practical strategies, and unapologetic truth bombs that help families reclaim their voice, restore respect, and raise actual grown-ups.

When she's not writing or coaching parents, Angela can be found courtside (or on her couch) cheering for Steph Curry, Draymond Green, and Giannis Antetokounmpo — three athletes whose discipline and grit inspire her "no shortcuts, play defense, trust your shot" approach to parenting and life.

Learn more at **AngelaSaint.com** and join the movement to build homes full of love, boundaries, and respect that travels.

RESOURCES FOR PARENTS

If you found strength, clarity, or a calm spine in these pages, here are your next steps:

Download the 5 Boundary Scripts (Free & Instant)
Real-life scripts for teen attitudes, adult child disrespect, money boundaries, and emotional resets.

Listen to the Calm Spine Audio Mini-Series
Short audio pep talks for heated moments when you need grounding fast.

Join the Email List
Weekly boundary boosters, parenting courage notes, and early previews of upcoming books.

Follow the Series
- Book 2 — *Boundaries Without Bitterness*
- Book 3 — *Love Without Losing Yourself*
- Book 4 — *The Gray-Haired Toddler Stage*
- Book 5 — *Earn Your Crown*

Your growth is your child's greatest inheritance.

JOIN THE CALM SPINE CLUB

Your home deserves leadership, clarity, and peace — and you don't have to learn it alone.

Inside the **Calm Spine Club**, you receive:
- Monthly 90-minute workshops
- Replay access
- Weekly Boundary Boosters
- Script Library
- 10% off 1:1 sessions
- Private Q&A through the "Ask Miss Dee" channel
- A community of parents committed to raising respectful, grounded kids

The Club is where your consistency becomes transformation.

Visit **AngelaSaint.com/club** to join.

COMING NEXT: BOOK 2 — BOUNDARIES WITHOUT BITTERNESS

How to set limits with love, confidence, and zero guilt.

If Book 1 taught you how to stop bullying behaviors at home, Book 2 teaches you how to hold boundaries without losing yourself.

Inside Book 2 you'll discover:
- How to stop over giving
- How to detach from adult kids with grace
- How to say "no" without a speech
- How to break the guilt cycle
- How to reset respect in relationships
- How to honor your needs without apology

The journey continues — and so does your transformation.

CLOSING BLESSING

May your spine grow steadier,
Your home grow calmer,
Your boundaries grow kinder,
And your confidence grows louder.

You are not raising children —
you are raising future adults.
And you are doing better than you think.

With gratitude, strength, and love,
Angela Saint

BEFORE YOU GO — I'VE GOT A GIFT FOR YOU.

If you made it to this page, then you're serious about raising a child with respect, resilience, and emotional maturity. And you deserve tools that make the journey lighter, calmer, and way more joyful.

So I created something just for you:

The Calm Spine Printable Pack — FREE for Readers

Inside you'll find:

The Calm Spine Scorecard

The Monthly Reset Tracker

The Parent Pause Checklist

The Emotional Storm Recovery Sheet

The 10-Second Reset Card

And a few surprises I tucked in for encouragement

These printables turn the lessons from this book into daily habits that actually stick.
Fun. Simple. No guilt. No chaos.

Download your pack instantly at:

AngelaSaint.com/Calm Spine Tools

Print them. Post them. Stick them on the fridge.
Use them as a mirror, a guide, and a pep talk on the days when parenting feels less like a calling and more like a cardio routine.

This is your next step toward the home you've been praying for — peaceful, structured, loving, and led with a calm spine.

I'm proud of you.
Let's keep growing together.

— **Angela Saint**

www.ingramcontent.com/pod-product-compliance
Lightning Source LLC
Chambersburg PA
CBHW021139160426
43194CB00007B/627